INGER SUSAEG

The Secrets of the Psyche

Connections between body, mind and feelings

All rights of distribution, including via film, radio, and television, photomechanical reproduction, audio storage media, electronic data storage media, and the reprinting of portions of text, are reserved.

Printed in the European Union on environmentally friendly, chlorine- and acid-free paper.

© 2019 novum publishing

ISBN 978-3-99064-534-5
Editing: B.Ed (Hons) Julie Hoyle
Cover: Kenneth Kullman, Scandinavian Stockphoto
Cover design, layout & typesetting: novum publishing
Internal illustrations: see bibliography p.159

www.novum-publishing.co.uk

Contents

1 Introduction 7
2 Particles know 13
3 What is life? 19
4 Crosswise of time and space 25
5 Our cells are treasures 31
6 The nature of the soul 35
7 Where in the body do the different
   feelings create pain? 41
   The head 44
   The throat 44
   The upper back/chest and shoulders 45
   Heart area/chest/upper part of back/arms 45
   Solar plexus/the belly/the back 46
   The hip area 47
   The thighs 47
   The knees and the feet 48
   The body's energy field in flow, side view 50
   The body's energy field in flow, front view 51
8 What makes life work against us? 52
9 A new approach 60
10 The Keys of Liberation 62
   Key number 1 Realising what we actually feel ... 62
   Key number 2 Forgiving the feelings 64
   Key number 3 Love for oneself 68
   Key number 4 To let go means to leave behind ... 71
11 The inner child 74
12 Parents and children 81
13 Important features of the human nature 90
14 The relationship to ourselves and to each other .. 98
15 Irrational patterns 103
16 Emotional pain from earlier lives 112

17 Contracts we do with ourselves 118
18 Self-recognition is door-opening 122
19 How to find the memory? 126
    The everyday feelings 126
    The list of where the different feelings
    are stuck in the body 126
    Regression – to travel back in time 127
    Relaxing exercise and introduction to regression 127
    To travel into the pain by the help of the thoughts 129
    Album 131
    Pendulum 132
20 Grief and how to relate to grief 135
21 Practical use of the Keys of Liberation 139
22 Going on 147
23 The good life 150
Explanations of terms and information about
   names that are marked with an asterisk 155
Pictures for the book 159

1 Introduction

During the last hundred years several invisible phenomenon have come into being, devices that weren't thinkable before they emerged as a result of technological development. This started with the ordinary telephone, then came the radio, then television. Now we take mobile phones, computers and broadband for granted without giving many thought to the technology behind the devices.

We experience ourselves in the same way. Most of us take life for granted and assume that it continues for us until the day comes when something doesn't work. We cannot just replace ourselves, like we do with mobile phones. Science actually knows a highly developed technology behind a variety of invisible energy forms that we benefit from and enjoy, while the 'technology' behind what makes us alive and creates life, seems to be a mystery. Perhaps it may be wise to know what causes a crash in our machinery?

When we reflect on it, we can all observe that there is an energy giving life everywhere in what is alive. If humans, animals and plants didn't have life energy, it would be as if we were made of stone. Immeasurable? Let's put it this way: Life energy isn't measurable by metric units, but it is to a large extent measurable in terms of larger or smaller presence. Isn't it time we find "the technology" behind the phenomenon "the human being", and do research on which measurement units can be used on life energy? I think we need to lift our eyes and look in new directions for answers.

From time immemorial, human beings have become ill without understanding why. Many are the ways and methods we have used to try to make us well. Nevertheless, neither the ways of thinking and research in the West nor Asian philosophy and methods have managed to break the 'health code': What is causing pain and illness to occur in the body?

The purpose of this book is to show a new approach to the human being, based upon a different way of thinking. I want to show how we can achieve new possibilities for a better life and health by logical reasoning and by observing life and nature. The understanding I present is based upon studies of life energy and on observations of humans and experiences that I have done in self-development work.

In 2004 I developed a method I call 'The Keys of Liberation'. By applying the method, which is described towards the end of the book, I have gained knowledge about how the life energy operates in the body and what makes pain occur. To start with I got insights through experiences by working through memories and by letting go of emotional pain. I could see and understand how emotional wounds created negative thoughts. They disappeared when I worked through painful memories.

After a while, I received requests from people interested in the work I was doing. By guiding them towards the reasons for their pain and problems and by teaching them how to use the method, I discovered that most people had similar patterns and the same possibilities to set themselves free from pain. Gradually, I got a clearer picture of how the body, the thoughts and the feelings function together. By working actively with myself and with others, I became aware of a number of factors that relate to human health. Therefore, this book also presents some causalities that I found through my work.

As a patient you may experience what doctors call some illnesses and pain as psychosomatic. In other words, doctors realize that the psyche influences the physical body, without being aware of the connection between them. In my opinion it is time that this field is explored with new eyes so that it's possible to build bridges between medicine and psychology. Humans are whole individuals, not biological devices equipped with thoughts and feelings.

When I started to understand this, I asked myself the question: Could the pain in my arms have anything to do with my thoughts and feelings? Having reflected on this, I realised that it is obvious, but something we rarely have learned anything about. I am sure you have had pain in your stomach once you were afraid? Then it isn't so strange, if pain in another part of the body indicates another painful feeling?

The many directions within natural medicine that have showed up during the last years show that many human beings want to take responsibility for their own health in new ways. The fact that there is a connection between the feelings and the body is no new thing. There are several methods working on the connection between the body and the psyche, for example The Rosen Method* and applied kinesiology* that find answers by touch and contact with the body while they ask questions to the mind and feelings.

The exploration I have done on this area has another approach than traditional nature scientific ways. I have searched for other ways of thinking. I have found answers by asking questions about existence and by observing my own life. I have concluded that it's the thinking about health, about how the body and psyche function, that needs to change. The answers are not complicated, but different. They are not found by studying books or long winded theories. It has been a benefit for me not to have read much about medicine, psychology or biology. If I had, I think my mind would have got stuck. The challenge is to set free the thought and disconnect both from things you have learned and society's perceptions of what is true. To get there, I have let go of reading books and I have only rarely looked at TV or listened to the radio for a long period. We are actually much more influenced by other people's thoughts than we are aware of and not least of all, by the media. This is probably caused by human nature's tendency to look up to someone who knows better.

Everybody can follow my chain of thought because the answers I have found are based on general knowledge, logic reasoning – and human experiences and considerations. Everybody is open to the fact that we need new directions to find answers to the questions about health that still lie unanswered. Therefore, I invite both you who are trained in the health sector and public in general to take time to observe and reflect together with me. It's important to detach from old thoughts about how you think things are.

What is important is that you don't start asking for proof as soon as you read assertions that don't fit with your perception about how things are. The first thing is; there are many things that are impossible to prove. This is mostly because it's not possible to measure consciousness, the way we are used to think. What I have found, which is important to underline, is that you get growing insights and certainty about how existence function, as you recognize, release and let go of painful emotions and related limiting thoughts. Secondly, there are several established truths that are built upon assumptions that were done long before the atom and quantum physics were born. Such truths aren't necessarily true, even if they represent the public opinion.

This started when I decided not to take the happy pills the doctor gave me when I got anxiety. I decided instead to study my thoughts and feelings. As I observed myself, I discovered which thoughts triggered feelings that activated pain in my stomach. It led to a long journey into the fantastic mysteries of the body, or better said, the soul's and the cells' secrets and wisdom. If you have experienced diarrhea when you are nervous, you have experienced the direct connection between your thoughts, feelings and body. What I have found, is that most pain in the body comes from emotional pain. The understanding I have developed, is based upon experiences that have convinced me that our feelings are reflected in the entire body. If you actively use the method I present, you will also develop growing insights, not only about yourself, but about life in general.

Both physical and mental distress is a major challenge for health authorities today. The method and ways of thinking described here, work great when you have a pain to work with on your own. With patience and dedicated effort you can free yourself from both physical and mental problems of a milder type. It is possible to work on your own to free yourself from pain. I have not experienced any kind of danger in facing your feelings the way this method entails. You may experience very strong emotions that you never knew you had, but this also provides an insight into the necessity of doing so. This is because through using this method you understand how things are connected. I also warmly recommend physicians or psychologists to use these keys in your own lives. This will give you valuable information for your own professional practice as well as your personal development.

You might think that it's a part of someone's personality to have emotional outbursts. I partially agree. If tempers are positive and don't affect others, we can live well with strong feelings. However, if the feelings make us think negative thoughts, cause us to be afraid, cause us to accuse and attack or make us feel like losers or victims, it is a great advantage to realize that we can get rid of them.

Many books claim that positive intentions work like creating energy. When we repeat thoughts about something we want and feel confident that it will happen, it shall be a reality. I agree partially. However, there is much in the way that prevents our thoughts from creating what we want. Through the work with myself, I discovered how we create many of the events in life that we seemingly cannot control. They are created by subconscious thoughts. My experience though, is that the subconscious is a treasure. There are the patterns that form the basis of how we perceive ourselves, which in turn shape our lives. This book provides a perspective on how to access the hidden feelings and your own subconscious. Those patterns often seem limiting because they are created by situations where we feel hurt, betrayed, devalued, etcetera. By grabbing what you really feel through your everyday life, doors begin to open to a new and richer life, and thereby to better health.

2 Particles know

It is more than 100 years since physicists presented how physical reality consists of atoms, which in turn consist of even smaller particles. Atomic structures have become part of general knowledge. We learnt in school that matter consists of tiny particles, electrons, spinning around nuclei. We have learned that atoms have different numbers of electrons from element to element, but the electrons are the same in all the elements.

The elements can be related to each other in different chemical compounds so that the atoms bind to each other by the electrons spinning in several atoms simultaneously, forming molecules. The electrons do this by spinning alternately in each element. They thus form completely different substances in this way. The same particles can form any substance which consists of molecules in addition to forming elements. *In other words, one single particle has the ability of spinning in and forming all elements and all chemical compounds between them.*

Atomic physics explains that the particles are so tiny and the spinning patterns so big in relation to them that actually, matter mostly consists of vibrating "space". They say that it is the particles' spin that make us perceive matter as firm. It means that even the *physical body is only seemingly firm matter.*

Here is a concrete example: What makes one and the same electron spin in an oxygen atom when it contributes to constitute oxygen and then to spin in an iron compound when it has got inside of the body? This happens in our body constantly when the iron in the blood binds itself to the oxygen of the air we breathe in so that the blood can transport oxygen to all the cells.

What make electrons in an atom cooperate with electrons in the other atoms so that they form molecules together? The answer I have found is just as logic as it is amazing:

They **know** how!

The particles that constitute the natural elements must have *knowledge* about how they form them, or matter would not exist. All particles must actually have knowledge about all the elements and all the compounds between them, or they could not react with each other the way they do. By having general knowledge we can all observe that particles are fantastic at cooperating in getting things to happen in creation. This happens not least in the human body, where the constituents are dividing and form new compounds continuously.

I have found that particles' conscious qualities are a precondition for life.

Think carefully about the logic of my reasoning. If particles have the ability to remember and think, it changes the entire perception of reality, right? I mean that it's because we consist of conscious particles, that we are able to think! However, because our thoughts are so obvious for us, we have not had the ability until now to see and understand our own nature.

I hope that my contribution to a change of thinking with this book may inspire scientific environments to open up to the fact that particles have conscious qualities. Especially since the early 1700s, science and laymen have been used to reason about existence in a "mechanical" way. Research and development concerning the body and the psyche isn't much influenced by the atom and quantum physics' non-linear thinking, even if it's more than a hundred years since the knowledge about the atom was presented. In my opinion, that is one of the reasons that development on Earth, dominated by a western influence, seems to have run into a track of increased materialism and superficiality.

I have reflected a lot on the nature of existence and I would like to invite many different disciplines to find new answers to the phenomenon in existence that we still haven't found answers to. I suggest a few questions right here that you can reflect on relating to my assumption: What makes your eyes able to see? What make your ears able to perceive sound? What make you able to perceive smell? What make you able to taste? What makes you able to think? What does that instrument with which you think consist of?

We can observe that all life develops on tiny units that contain all the information about the individual. Seeds become plants and trees, fertilized roe becomes thousands of fish and fertilized egg cells become animals and humans. What happens with a seed, with a living individual, doesn't happen by chance, but it develops exactly *that* individual. In most cases the individuals are not alike but have the possibility of variations. So how can the information about the plant, about the animal, about the human, be stored in such small units? The answer is again just as logical as amazingly simple, when we think in a new way. The particles that the seed consists of must be able to remember!

Particles must know how that particular kind of tree develops and what it looks like! For example, that it has needles and not leaves, that it is green all through the winter and doesn't loose its leaves. I mean it can only be the way it is because the particles have the ability to remember information about this single individual in nature when they have started to constitute a cell structure. There must be some kind of programming in the particles at the very start that makes them able to form life on Earth. To make everything able to develop the way it does, *all particles must know everything about how all life develops!* It is the same with the elements. All particles must know about how all species develop from the smallest units, because all life withers, dies and dissolves to start growing again from the seed level. The particles that then arrive from the sun light and from the soil to enable the growth of new individuals must have knowledge about how they collect information from the particles in the seed to form new cells in the specific species.

Think about this: The big pine tree that grows from the seed in the cone consists of millions of cells, which again consist of particles that all must know how they form the pine tree or they aren´t able to cooperate in creating it. In other words, what one particle knows about the pine, all particles that it consists of know! The seed must contain all information about how the entire tree is created because the seed cells divide and become two cells and the two divide again and so on to become the tree. This is what we know from biology. The cells must have knowledge about how they form bark and pine needles as well as the stem and how it all fits together as a whole. The way I see it, it's the particles' consciousness that makes it possible for the cells to do what they do.

We know that a tree contains more and more particles as it grows. We know that the plants get energy from the sun light, which provides for development and growth. It is likely that trees contain particles that originate both from the soil and the sun. The particles are thus from very different sources and have the ability to cooperate to form new structures.

Similarly with the human body. Most people have experienced that skin can peel off and repair itself. The same happens when we get a wound. The cells largely find their original structure after an injury. So the cells' qualities show that it's logical that there is consciousness in our cells. Again I suggest that the particles that the cells consist of have the ability of being conscious. When it comes to the human body, the particles must come from somewhere to form new cells. Here too, it's probable that the cells are formed both by the food we eat and by particles that have their origin in sun light and in electric light. I believe that science communities can use these ideas as starting points for new research.

Actually particles show many fascinating things about existence when we take time to reflect. The particles must cooperate for matter to be able to exist, right? Thus, cooperation is a basic quality in the smallest building blocks we consist of. Can we conclude from this that cooperation is one of the basic qualities in our human nature?

If so what more qualities do particles have that are worth noticing? Try to imagine how it would be to be a particle, spinning in an atom! Every single particle must *trust* that the others do their job. Trust seems to be a prerequisite to make particles able to form matter. It resembles the trust we as humans have that everybody drives on the correct side of the road.

The next thing to come to mind when I imagine how it is to be a particle, is that all the others are like myself – that we are all equal. We do the same jobs and are dependent on each other to make existence function. A quality needed to make a society function as well! Still, the most important thing I have discovered when imagining being a particle, is that they must have the ability to communicate with each other. This is logical because all particles have the ability to do all the same tasks. Like in the example about the pine tree we can observe; what one particle knows, all the particles that form the same tree must know.

This alerts me to even more qualities that particles have: Persistence and acceptance of their situation. This little reflection shows that changing perspective about particles can show the way for a new way of thinking, not only within science, but in life in general. If we are conscious because particles are conscious, it is our basic nature to cooperate, to trust each other, to communicate, to see each other as equal and to be persistent and accepting. Assumptions about particle consciousness make completely new perspectives grow forth.

Many new answers become close when we think this way. To get there we must be willing to change our attitudes, not only to ourselves as beings and what we believe in, but to existence in its entirety. What we need to see, is that life is not linear and mechanic, but multi-dimensional. In our body there is much going on in addition to the atomic structure, the "vibrating space" that we consist of, phenomenon that no one has found explanations to within science. Pain for example. In the next chapter we will approach this challenge from a new angle.

3 What is life?

What is the difference between a human body and a sculpture? There must be 'something' that makes us human beings live, whilst things around us are «dead» and static. When we study this with philosophical eyes, we find that growth is what divides. It is development. It is movement. It is propulsion. From this, we can conclude that there is something in the human, in the animal and in the flower that is not in stone and metal. This 'something' must be there in addition to the atomic and molecular structure. We remember what we learned in science lessons; it is energy that provides propulsion and movement. In other words, this 'something' must be a kind of energy.

As we see life energy is easily evident when we ask questions about existence. There is no doubt that it's there but it's a riddle for me that science, until now seems to have neglected this. Where medical science stands today, it seems as if life energy is seemingly invisible because we are used to taking it for granted. As long as we look for something we can measure by an instrument, we may need to search for a long time but what if we ask: What kind of energy is providing propulsion? Gasoline? Coal? The mechanical thinking keeps us stuck in our old thinking. The prevailing thinking may say that food is the energy that gives propulsion. Yes, it is, in relation to the biological devices we are, but if we think non-mechanical, and think about ourselves as the wonderful versatile beings that we are; what is then the driving force in human beings?

It is our feelings and thoughts!

Our feelings make us want to do something and not something else. It is our thoughts that make us able to reflect, reason and draw conclusions. We do that, among other things based on feelings. It's our feelings that make us like something so that we develop in one direction and not in another. It is our feelings that make us grow and bloom! I have found that it is primarily our feelings that are the driving force for life itself. From that I have drawn the conclusion – and discovered by my own self-development work, that the life energy must be some kind of feeling energy. A basic energy form that we haven't explored because we take it for granted? Because our feelings are a subjective, private part of the human that cannot be measured or weighed?

It is actually rather obvious, and we have all experienced it: Negative feelings lead to negative thoughts that reduce our energy levels. When we are depressed, we don't want to do anything at all and then we have very little propulsion. Positive feelings and thoughts make us happy and give us energy to express and develop.

To find out more about what life energy really is, I have approached it through the following reasoning. All human beings all over the world have life energy whatever religion, culture or nation they belong to. Life energy simply lets life unfold whatever human beings do. Not even humans who kill other humans loose the life energy so that they die. From this, I have concluded that life energy is an accepting energy.

Another feature that everybody can observe: Life energy doesn't take side in conflicts. It is in all human beings, even in those who are at war with each other. It is in other words a neutral, non-judging energy or humans who do bad things to one another would loose their life energy.

Thus it is up to us to choose how we use the gift that life is. It is we humans who judge. Why do we do that, you may ask. That's exactly what this book is about. I have found that the emotional wounds that we carry along make us create conflicts, criticize and judge each other.

Think about this: Even if we do something criminal or stupid, our heart doesn't stop beating. Our body continues to live, seemingly as before, even if we do terrible things. However, only seemingly… because most people are affected by the fact that they are doing something that harms or hurts others. The energy that sustains the body is the same, while our emotions, and thus our thoughts, change. Guilt, despair, shame, fear, self-criticism or sorrow of what we did would affect our whole life. When someone continues to have life energy, even after committing awful acts such as killing, we can characterize the life energy as forgiving … otherwise the person would die immediately – or shortly thereafter?

Let's do a thought experiment.
If someone you know well…
Accepts you just the way you are…
Lets you unfold just the way you want…
Allows you to be who you are without judging you…
Forgives you when you do stupid things…

What do they do then? They love you without demands. Unconditional love. That is the way we can describe the nature of life energy. An energy that gives and gives life. Which continues to let life on Earth grow and develop. These considerations all together have made me draw the conclusion that the basic life energy in a human being is love.

Love is the driving force in life! Sure, that fits with the perception of most of us. Perhaps that is why we long for love if we don't have it?

As I have worked with these issues, I have come to the opinion that the life energy contains joy. I have done so based on observations related to my work as drama teacher. An exercise where I ask the participants to fill themselves with joy while they are asked to walk around and look down on the floor stooping their necks, is almost impossible to carry out. They just have to move and become full of laughter. Try it! When the participants get the instruction to feel depressed and simultaneously walk with a straight back and easy and open posture, they have big problems in carrying that out too. By doing this, they discover something essential: Feelings are situated in the entire body and the body's natural condition is to be happy. A happy human being feels the need to be so with the entire body. Both by my own development work and by guiding others, I have discovered a quivering pleasure when a trauma* is released and a negative thought pattern is gone. It also indicates that the energy of life contains joy.

As I have worked with these issues, I have discovered another aspect of the life energy. I think it contains joy. This opinion is based on observations related to my work as a drama teacher. An exercise where I ask the participants to fill themselves with joy while they walk around looking at the floor and stoop their necks, is almost impossible to do. They simply must move and many of them just have to laugh. Try it! Similarly when the participants get the order to be sad whilst walking with a straight back and open and easy posture, they have big problems in carrying out that exercise. Through this they discover something crucial in themselves: The feelings are situated in the entire body and the body's natural condition is to be happy. A happy human being feels the need of being it with the entire body. Both in my own release work and when guiding others I have discovered a quivering joy when a trauma* is released and a negative thought pattern is gone. It also indicates that the life energy contains joy.

An experience that made me convinced about another aspect of the nature of the life energy, is an experience I had during a meditation. I have hardly meditated at all during my life so the event I refer to is unique. The task I had was to meditate on a flower and I chose a coltsfoot when it awakens to life at the roadside in the spring. I closed my eyes and sat a long while trying to imagine that I was the coltsfoot… and suddenly I was it! I felt like the thick, leaf-shaped stem and the beaming, yellow crown. I was filled with a tremendous sense of love by being a coltsfoot, joy to delight those who came on the road and saw me – and the pride of being a beautiful coltsfoot! – A powerful experience that taught me a lot about existence, to which I have related in many cases later. The experience was so strong that I do not doubt that it contains true information – even if it was subjective.

Therefore I am convinced that life energy, not only contains love and joy, but pride also. Think how proud young children can be at what they manage… and how sorry they are if we do not have time to look at them or what they want to show us. I think that this also underlines a feature of the energy that life is. I believe this because young children have not been able to limit their life energy because of emotional wounds, like so many adults have.

Another important feature that I have observed with life energy: Every single moment we have the possibility to live a new moment – and then a new. It is up to every one of us to choose to do things differently every single moment. The life energy is there for us in the present. Physical life is actually only being lived in the present. Everything that has been were experiences and memories. What come are plans, hopes and dreams. However, everything that is behind us also contains the wounds that form the experience of the present. Therefore our thoughts contain, not only optimism and a wealth of ideas, but limitations formed by the wounds, like lack of trust, prejudices and worry for what might happen.

My studies of life energy have shown me what makes life difficult for humans are small and big painful memories. They make us hold on to the past so that they prevent us from life joy and life multitude. It means that the wounds we carry prevent us from being the way life energy is, which is love, joy and pride. Can you see, that it is the painful feelings that we carry from the situations in our lives that prevent life energy so that we get ill and eventually die?

My discovery actually is, that illness occurs as a result of feelings that have got 'stuck' because they are not been worked through and released but suppressed. Our nature is to be pleasant, so we'd rather not feel the bad feelings, but I've found that is what we have to learn, if we want to stay healthy and live a long life.

When I discovered what I have described above, I had already for a long time worked to love myself. I had read it and knew intuitively that it is important, but I didn't realize at that time why it is so important. Within the last two years, after I understood that particles are conscious, I have had several aha-experiences. I have found that the key to what life energy is, lies in every single cell. There must be programmings on all cells that make them contain love when life starts. The driving force behind growth and development is already present in the fertilized egg cell. From biology we know that it divides and the two cells have the same qualities as the first. Then the cells continue to divide and after a certain number of divisions they have the ability to do different functions. At the same time, in each of them there is a kind of self-preservation / energy that causes them to continue to grow, develop, cooperate, to renew, repair and enable cell structure.

Based on all these observations and conclusions, I believe that life energy is self-love in every single cell.

4 Crosswise of time and space

We are used to perceiving ourselves and each other as being limited by our bodies. Nevertheless, we use thoughts and feelings when we communicate and think about other people, do we not? Has it ever occurred to you that thoughts and feelings extend far outside the body irrespective of time and space? We are used to thinking linearly and mechanically about ourselves. Most people might think that thoughts are located inside our heads, but are they? I mean, when you think about your sister on at the other side of town, the energy from your thought is there with her. When you think about that nice holiday you had with your sweetheart last year, your thought energy may still be in the apartment where you stayed on the Mediterranean. I have discovered that conscious thoughts are energy impulses, which are sent out of our mind so that they can reach the people we think about. Most of us have experienced at some point that someone who we have just thought about, calls us on the telephone. This is an example of how thoughts can reach others even if they are far away. Usually a fleeting thought isn't enough to reach the minds of the people we think of, but if we concentrate and visualize and feel good about the person, I think there is a greater chance. What happens then, is that our soul seeks contact and is able to communicate with the person's soul, which may happen across huge distances.

The example with the students in the previous chapter is not the only the way. Not only the example with the students in the previous chapter, shows the way. If you reflect on it, you have many experiences showing that feelings are felt in the entire body. When we say we get goose pimples from something we experience, it's feelings that influence the body. When we blush and suddenly get very warm, the same happens. When we feel love for a human being that is far away geographically, we may feel warmth spreading throughout our entire body.

Through our thoughts we actually move outside of our bodies more or less all the time. If we perceive ourselves as body, thoughts and feelings holistically, our reality and experience reaches far beyond our physical body. It is our way of thinking that keeps us stuck in an image of ourselves that is limited to the body. When we collect information to make us healthy, we need to move back beyond (crosswise) time and space, back to the memories that created the pain in the first place. Then we need to 'travel' by the help of our thoughts and feelings. Perhaps you need to travel back to your childhood, and most likely you lived in another place than you do now? Still, you can activate your feelings so that you can remember the place and the situations in detail. Then you can actually be there by your soul, even if the house might have been demolished! Your soul has a different perception of time than the mind has and I have discovered that to a certain degree it may see forward in time. It is the explanation for what we call 'déjà vu', a feeling of 'This is something I have experienced previously'.

After years of reflection, I feel that the most important thing to understand about human beings is: We live in physical bodies and experience ourselves on a timeline, concurrently as multi-dimensional, non-linear beings existing irrespective of time and space.

Gradually I have got used to using the term 'soul' about the part of us that represents our feelings. I have found that it is a type of conscious energy that has the ability to place itself inside the body's molecular space – the physical body. During work on the release of my painful feelings, I discovered that the soul has a timeless character.

You are your soul and it is you, but at the same time your soul has the ability to expand far outside your body. When you "travel" back to something you are thinking of, you can remember details, colors and even smells. Then your soul is back in the memory and experiences the situation again by being there. Simultaneously you are there with your mind's now-awareness because your mind is connected to the soul by the energy system that is situated around and through the body.

My experience is that the centre of the soul is in the middle of the chest. We have many "heart" expressions for feelings and I think you might agree that both love and grief can be felt physically in the heart. But the soul is simultaneously reflected in the cells of the body and particularly the face, especially the eyes and the mouth. Our soul is an extremely important part of us. Without soul we would not have the driving force to do anything, neither would we develop qualities and abilities. I have discovered that the soul consists of many components that represent different qualities and abilities.

The energy system of the human being (see page 49 and 50) contains thought and emotional energy which means our perceptions and feelings. The energy system is a fantastic system that is well known and variously described and applied within the

Chinese tradition, Hindu tradition and nature medicine. The energy is invisible to our physical eyes, but I have actually experienced seeing the energy channels with my inner eye. It is a communication system consisting of conscious energy ensuring that thoughts, feelings and physical body work together.

In the pictures it is presented diagrammatically as an egg-shaped field around the body, but in reality it is very flexible and dynamic. If you are a fearless, searching and open person that sees possibilities and wants to develop, your energy field is wide because your thoughts and feelings disperse in many directions. If you are worried and think limiting thoughts, your energy field is rather close to the body. What I have discovered by my work; when you release emotional pain, you may expand your field because you reduce fear and limiting thoughts.

When we move into another person's energy field, we may be influenced by their perceptions and they may be influenced by ours. This only happens if we are insecure or if someone wants to influence somebody else. However, it's the reason we intuitively want to sit alone on the bus and have a private zone we prefer to keep other people outside of.

The energy field contains patterns of reactions and ways of acting, which in turn have consequences for the people around us. Another way of saying this: The subconscious thoughts we think about ourselves and each other as a result of the wounds in our soul, are in the field around us. For example, if you, in a situation earlier in life experienced feeling you weren't sufficient, or that you weren't good enough, that perception is situated in your field as thoughts about yourself. *The sensational phenomenon I have found is that the subconscious thoughts in the energy field function as creating energy in the same way as conscious thoughts do.* This means that the humans around you in this example might perceive the subconscious thoughts you have about yourself so that you may experience new situations where you feel that you aren't sufficient and that you are not good enough in your own and other's eyes. It may make you compensate by trying to assert yourself in different ways. Or it may make you insecure and get complexes and even become a victim of bullying.

The energy field around us may also contain perceptions we pick up from others, from society and from the media. Trends occur both because our thoughts are communicated directly from field to field and because of what we see others do or have. Collective perceptions that we carry along from generation to generation also lie in the energy fields around us.

I experienced seeing and understanding more and more about how existence functions as I released painful feelings. By that I removed thoughts that limited me in understanding what is possible. The answers came to me as aha-experiences and sudden insights with a certainty that the insight I got was true. The challenge for me has been to explain this to the human beings around me, especially academics who demand that I must prove my findings in traditional ways. The answer is; we cannot prove these connections. They must be understood gradually as an individual human being experiences that this is the way it is. Nevertheless, I believe that it is possible to do research on these circumstances when you use another approach than scientific methods. I am certain that the collective perception about the nature of existence gradually will start changing as more and more people experience that the release of painful feelings opens doors to higher awareness.

During the last decades, self-development has become popular. Many people claim that it is a selfish trend, but everybody who has worked with their inner issues in this and similar ways, will agree that it is the opposite. To seize hold of your life means to be honest with yourself and to dare to face your weaknesses. It also means developing your strengths and using them positively, without being selfish. It has led to an increased awareness in many people who have released emotional wounds. The gathered knowledge about release thus becomes greater as every single one of us works to release our pain.

My experience is that our mind consists of particles that are connected to the universal particle consciousness. However, most of the time, we are not able to reach universal wisdom because of our painful emotions, which created limiting thoughts. We can only reach universal wisdom when being one with our soul. We can reach such a state by removing all pain from memories in the past, which have led to the limiting thinking. You may say it this way: If you release all negative feelings and limiting thoughts, you may obtain expanded consciousness (enlightenment), which means that you are able to expand your energy field and get new ideas and astonishing answers from the universal wisdom. You would then be directly in contact with the universal consciousness.

5 Our cells are treasures

From experiences in working with myself and others I have discovered that the body has its own consciousness and its own language. It is continuously trying to tell us what is not in alignment with it or with the life energy. Unfortunate thought patterns create obstacles in the energy system so that the life energy in the cells becomes weaker. Thus one way we can find out what is hidden in the subconscious is by the signals of the body. All the cells in the body are actually living organisms with their own consciousness that cooperate with all the other cells. The body is a fantastic composition of components that are finely tuned to everything going on in your life. The amazing thing is that the cells in the body are a memory bank about everything you have experienced, good and bad. I discovered that the memories get stored in organs, muscles and tissues in the body and not in the brain. I understood it by moving my thought into physical pain, keeping it there until I got impulses as pictures, sensations or words.

One thing is important to underline: Your body is your own. You are the one having contact with it, not the doctor or the therapist. You know what is best for you when you really take time to feel. When you get to know your body this way and you understand the connections of your body, you will choose to find the reason of your discomfort on your own, rather than seeking help from doctors and therapists. Train your intuition; it is always at your body's wavelength, but rarely agreeing with what you find in books, magazines and newspapers. You can train it by using it and by finding out if what you feel is right.

You have developed your body through many good experiences of mastering and rejoicing since you were born. You know what it can take and when you need to take it easy. You know when you need to get in better shape. Don't let others tell you when you need a break – decide for yourself without pushing your body too hard. It is a fantastic friend and at the same time, it's you. However, we really need to go for it when we know we need exercise!

On my journey discovering the knowledge I am sharing with you, I discovered how we can communicate with the consciousness of the body. When I travel into my body by the help of my thoughts, I do it with naïve openness. We communicate easily when we are on the same wavelength. If you try this you need to let the part of your mind rest that tries to find solutions. That part of the mind will always suggest what you have learned already or what the culture or the media says. Nevertheless, your adult conscious mind needs to be present, but totally neutral. To find solutions, your mind needs to be open to all possibilities.

When I explore the body to find answers, the starting point is always some kind of discomfort. Maybe it's nervousness in my stomach or maybe it's a painful muscle. There may be a rash or just an acute pain somewhere. I simply move into the area of the body and ask the cells in the uncomfortable part what they want to tell me. When I get an impulse, I reflect on whether the answer is right for me. Sometimes I continue by asking more questions and I may get several words that help me to understand what the pain is about. One of the things I have found out about cells, is that they love gratitude. Cells respond when you thank them.

It is actually logical to communicate with our own cells. If you feel gratitude to your cells daily and talk to them with loving words, you will notice that they respond. Your body deserves to get the best treatment you can give it, not only physically, but as your thoughts and feelings. It is there for you all the time. It also means that you have a responsibility to let your body be pleasant by dressing comfortably, not too tight and sufficiently so that you don't get cold. The clothes you choose need to be correctly related to your work also, so that you manage to do what you are supposed to. It isn't very clever to dress in ways that arouse indignation in others. Both in fact influence the wellbeing of your cells i.e. your own wellbeing. All human beings can improve their relationship to their body. If you feel that you have done something you regret for example, that you have pushed yourself too hard, you can ask your body for forgiveness! It also means that you need to realize when your body has come to the point that it needs rest. When you have used too tight shoes, for example, you can ask your cells of forgiveness… and decide never to use those shoes again. In this and similar ways you will get a good and close relationship to your body.

I have started to massage my feet daily and I can recommend this as a good investment. I speak to them with gratitude whilst giving them the massage. Reflexologists say that the feet reflect the entire body and I can confirm that by my own experiences. When you massage your feet, it is as if you give a massage to your entire body!

I have noticed that when I am in a good mood and grateful to life and everything I have, my face gets smooth and I feel that I shine. It's a direct connection between our inner and outer life. I am sure that you see many examples in your own life when you take time to reflect.

Do you reflect upon where the food you eat comes from? Can you see; by assuming that particles have conscious qualities, we can think in a new way related to food and our body? Everything we take into our bodies comes from nature, which means that most atoms in our bodies come from plants and animals. The plants and animals consist of particles having their origins in soil, sunlight and water. Inside our bodies, the particles transform the food, not only to energy but continually renewing our cells. They are cleaved into single particles that know exactly where to go. Think of it; a particle of food finds its way through the digestion system to become a particle in a cell in your left thumb nail… isn't that fantastic? When you reflect on it, there is no other way this can happen, than that all the particles know what to do and self organise.

I have discovered that particles also respond to love and gratitude through time and space. My theory is that all particles that constitute living cells have a kind of knowledge about the entire creation. The kind of internal connection that particles must have to be able to form life has been too difficult to understand for the linear mind because we haven't developed ways of thinking that include particles' consciousness. A way to find out about an assumption like this is to communicate with the particles. Our thought is actually a communication with particles and so are our feelings. Thus our thoughts and feelings are the energies that make things happen.

6 The nature of the soul

Many years ago I got a glimpse of a book about the issue 'near-death-experiences' in a bookshop window and felt strongly that I just had to go inside to buy it. It was an interesting book and at the back of it were many literary references. Eventually I read several books about the same issue. They described how many people who had been at the threshold of death had experienced how they could remember hovering out of their body and meeting beings in human form in another type of existence. They felt extremely light and happy in that condition. Some even experienced that they were able to move out of their body, through walls and see people in other rooms. Others described how they could see their body below and then move through a tunnel that led to another world where they met relatives who were dead. They described that they felt very heavy when they woke up in their physical body afterwards. When humans experience such conditions, they *are* their soul. I mean that near-death-experiences are valuable even for science when we open up to the fact that the human consists of both consciousness and physical matter. Even if experiences are subjective, they are real for those who experience them and they tell us much about the nature of human beings. Most people that have experienced a near-death-experience say that it made them change their way of life. Therefore, there is something for us all to learn from it. A human that experiences such a condition, experiences it through their feelings. I have found that the souls of those of us who have lived before, usually have the ability to move out of the body during meditation and sleep. However, many people haven't lived earlier lives and for them it's difficult to understand that the soul may live many lives.

The knowledge I refer to in this book has grown forth in me through experiences by releasing memories from many former lives. If I hadn't been willing to realise that I have lived before, I would not have been able to release the anxiety that occurred in my life at the end of my forties. It turned out to have its roots in a life where I was stoned because I opposed the church and public opinion. The anxiety disappeared the moment I understood the connection to what triggered it in this life, which was my growing spiritual interest, whilst simultaneously working in an academic environment. At that point of time, I had read the books I mentioned above and thus I had related to earlier lives for a while. I was convinced that I had lived several times before. It made me have a relaxed attitude to death and I often expressed my views among my colleagues. To be engaged in spiritual matters wasn't quite acceptable with some of them, so my soul got a growing, irrational fear.

Humans are different from each other. Through my work I have discovered that it doesn't only depend on genes and how we look. It has to do with our souls' different age, origin and composition. Some people have lived many lives whilst others are living their soul's first life. Besides, there are different soul families having different compositions of soul qualities. That is why humans are as different as we are.

It isn't usual to remember earlier lives, but some people have the ability to remember even the details from earlier lives, when they relax deeply. What they can tell is in my opinion very useful information for science and society. Even if the information that comes forth in such subjective experiences is emotional experiences seen with the soul's eyes, I think such information is an important contribution that can supply and adjust historians' views. It depends on the eyes that see and the rules that the humans have made for themselves, whether this information may be able to shed light upon the past. I mean such former lives experiences can become fantastic additions for archeologists and historians in the years to come. Science simply must open up to the fact that humans are beings that cannot be measured and compared by linear methods only. The researchers must start relating to our true nature and no longer deny the part of us that the soul represents. The soul is the reason for illness and of course it is subjective because pain occurs in the single human being's meeting with life. It is to a large extent important to make us understand the wholeness of creation.

When an old soul has incarnated and is inside a newborn child, it may bring many memories from its earlier life. The soul sees him- or herself as experienced, but simultaneously as innocent and helpless inside the small child. At birth, the soul may perceive everything going on in the baby's life, even outside of the body. In the book 'Life before Life' by the American psychiatrist Helen Wambach*, based upon a large number of people's regressions* back to the moment of birth, some people tell about how they could read the mother's and doctor's and midwife's thoughts. So don't think small children don't understand what we say! To start with, some even know what we think. It seems though, that souls who are reborn soon forget their past.

As a child grows up, there will be episodes that *remind the soul about painful situations from earlier lives.* They may trigger feelings from memories that are stored in the body. There may be painful situations that he or she didn't release in an earlier life. On such occasions the child has much stronger feelings than what would be expected, because the soul cries about what happened a long time ago also. The child hasn't the ability to understand this and the pain becomes the basis for part of the child's self-perception. This doesn't need to be that way for ever. It means that it is just human nature to develop that way. As youth and adult we can work through and release pain from earlier lives as well as from this life.

I have discovered; when there isn't any old soul incarnating in a newborn child, it gets the parents' soul qualities through their love for the baby. Therefore it's extremely important to give love and care to newborns. Every single cell responds to the care they receive. All positive stimulation that we give lovingly and with patience during the first living years, forms the child's personality.

Lately I have become aware that it is usual that great grandparents, and sometimes grandparents incarnate as the family's children. The tradition of calling the children the ancestors' names probably comes from this soul practice. The soul of the great grandparent is close to the energy field of couples who expect a baby and give impulses to their minds about calling the child their name. Actually, I think this is unfortunate because then the soul will easily remember the life they lived before. They might feel old whilst still being children. The life we live here and now is what is important.

Today I know much more than what I knew at the time I started to search for answers. The soul is not only connected to the physical body. It is connected to a body of another type of energy (see picture below), filling the same space as the physical body. It's an ethereal energy, invisible for the physical eye, where the particles are spinning in other ball patterns than in atoms. The ethereal energy actually forms a copy of the physical body. It is to some extent dependent on one's self-perception as the ethereal body also is connected to the energy system and the soul's perception of oneself.

The ethereal body is the invisible body we go on living with when we die. Today I am able to connect to dead people. It happens like this: When I get the image of someone in my inner eye and I suddenly start to think of them, I know that he or she wants to tell me something. I have no doubt that there is a life after death that can be both developing and joyful.

The energy system's task (page 49) is to connect the cells with our thoughts and feelings, or we would not function as whole beings. When we are newborn souls, our mind starts develop-

Ethereal particle spin
This is the way particles spin in the invisible, ethereal energy inside of every single living cell. The particles can spin in such spheres in greater or lesser density. This knowledge came to me when I had reached expanded consciousness by the help of the Keys of Liberation.
Similar images that have flat structure are found deep down in the old temple ruins in Abydos in Egypt, dated to be more than 6000 years old. It indicates that the ethereal energy was known for the ancient Egyptian culture. Leonardo da Vinci studied the geometric shapes that occur when you pull the lines between intersections in circles in a flat structure.

ing from our birth and continues to develop as long as we are learning. We can do that our entire life. The soul represents our feelings and vibrates both in our body and in our energy system. The nature of the soul is love and joy and many good qualities that vary from human to human. As we learn from our experiences up through life, we develop new qualities and our soul grows. When we come across situations where we are not met, we may experience it as difficult. It's because human souls have different origins and different compositions of qualities. Still, the soul's basic nature in most people is that it wants everybody to be good and kind, but what happens to us up through life, forms our personality the way we become as adults.

When we get hurt because someone we love ignores us, a cell in an area of the body gets another truth than the life energy! Instead of being love, the cell is saying the same as the soul: 'I am sad because he doesn't see me'. It gets another conviction than the positive life energy in the cell and it functions as a hindrance or obstacle to start with. If similar things happen so that the wound gets stronger, more cells in the same area start to say similar things. This is the way pain and eventually illness occurs. In this case, the pain would be felt in the chest and in the neck.

7 Where in the body do the different feelings create pain?

In recent years many of us have got acquainted with different types of nature medicine. You may have seen pictures of the meridian system* in the body that show the trigger points where acupuncture needles are placed to activate life energy? This is done to make the energy vibrate in areas where it is prevented and pain has occurred. The millennial Chinese medical knowledge has spread all over the world helping many people to ease pain. Such images show "the fine distribution" of the energy system in the body. My experience is that acupuncture eases the pain for a period, but to remove it, one needs to find what kind of feelings the pain represents.

The different feelings are related to different energy areas in the body. When we learn how the emotional pain manifests as physical pain, we can start to take responsibility for our health to a much larger degree. Physical ailments show the way to the emotional pain we carry. Therefore I have made a list of what I have found through my experiences.

The life energy in the cells is prevented by the soul's 'statements' that don't fit with its 'conviction' of *being love*. In computer language one would say that such feelings are not compatible with the life energy. Such emotional wounds remain as subconscious, repeating thoughts that are obstacles in the energy system. The body, which is a much more complicated 'machinery' than the computer, needs us to learn basic knowledge about how we can remove subconscious, denying sentences to make it function optimally in the long term. We need a user manual for life! When negative feelings and thoughts are repeated both consciously and subconsciously in muscles and organs, they cannot function optimally.

It is usual to have pain or discomfort several places in the body, related to the same memory. It is the way our feelings are related to the body. For example, you may be afraid that no one cares about you. Then you might have pain/trouble both in the stomach and in the throat because fear is situated in the stomach and the feeling that no one cares about you limits the life energy in the throat. You might have become angry with yourself, wounded and felt abandoned when someone left you. If this is repeated, you might get pain in the back, the chest and the arms. The anger is situated in the back, being wounded in the chest and the feeling of having been abandoned in the arms. Yet there is usually a main area that hurts related to a memory. If the painful feelings and thoughts lead to more experiences of a similar character, it causes more cells saying similar things and the pain gets stronger. Bodily pain occurs when our cells tell us repeatedly what hurts in our soul! We need to learn to listen to the cells' pain to hear what the soul wants to tell us. One way to find out is by practicing moving your thought into physical pain and listening to what the cells communicate.

Through my work I have found that the same types of feelings prevent the life energy in certain areas of the body of many of my clients as well as in me. From that I have concluded that feelings of the same kind prevent the life energy in the same body areas in all people.

There are variations, so that the list I describe here should not be used as a rule, but as a pointer to the direction in which one can apply to pinpoint problems and pain. There are surely more types of emotions and pain than those I have listed here. The emotion in question may have led to an obvious way of thinking for the person so that he or she believes it is the way it should be. Many times have I heard, 'Yes, but it's the way I am. I cannot do anything about it'. That's exactly what you can do. It may seem like a trifling matter, but when it repeats itself every day – especially if it affects both you and other people, it's really worth finding out how to get rid of feelings and beliefs that you don't need.

An example about a man who often got pain behind his shoulder blades when wanting to relax in the evening:

A man said to me: 'I cannot do anything about the fact that I am not able to let go of the thought of the weather ladies on TV who annoy me. Every time those affected women are showing themselves, I get so annoyed that I almost forget to look at the weather forecast'. The person admits that it is a problem that pulls him down. But how can he do anything about it? In this case the memory turned out to be from when he was 7 years old. He was sent to bed half an hour before regular bed time because his mother was going to a party and was busy putting on make-up when he wanted her attention to show her something he was proud of. It took only half an hour to sit down and realise exactly what he felt and to get the insights he needed. Since then, he has used the keys in his daily life and warmly recommends others do the same.

It is my hope that it will become normal to release feelings. – That release work will be a natural topic of conversation among friends and family. – That tears are just as natural as laughter and that we help each other when we see someone struggling. Below is a list of the areas that shows my experiences so far, about where in the body the different type of feelings prevent the life energy and thus create pain. These are the main areas, connected to the energy channels, see pictures page 49 and 50.

At the top of the head is the connection to the universal consciousness. There is only pain to a small extent in this area, but you may feel a tingling when you get insights in how everything fits together.

The head

This area isn't really related to feelings, but to all kinds of issues around not being willing to or not managing. Remember, it's *the soul* that doesn't manage to realise. For that reason it may be wise to use a pendulum related to pain in the head.

The jaw: Not willing to realise.

The rest of the head: Not willing to see/hear, not willing to understand. If you start to loose the ability to hear, for example, the problem might be that your soul isn't willing to listen! Something might have happened that your soul is not able to understand.

The throat

In front: You get pain here when you feel that no one cares about you. If you often get a sore throat, the reason may be similar. The energy to the thyroid gets reduced when you feel that no one cares about who you are, as the person you are. You might feel that you always must be present for all the others.

Right side of the throat: Self-criticism and the feeling that you judge yourself, to feel that others judge you. To feel run over, offended and/or abused.

Left side of the throat: Different kinds of feelings about not allowing oneself. To feel that someone has lied to you or fooled you. To feel that you have lied to others. To feel that you have been manipulated. To feel that you have fooled yourself.

At the back of the throat: To feel that you are not seen/heard/understood. To feel that you are not worth living. To feel that you are not worth love.

The upper back/chest and shoulders

In front, at the top of the breastbone: To feel that you don't deserve… love… life. To feel that you are not well.

At the top of the shoulders and in the tendons for the arms: To feel strongly that you want to manage something. In itself a positive intention, but when it is too strong, it results in pain. Instead you can practice having confidence that you manage what you have decided to do.

At the back; the three lower cervical vertebrae and the chest vertebrae: To feel too much responsibility and obligation, including what we feel we need to carry for others.

Heart area/chest/upper part of back/arms

In the middle of the chest: To feel grief, to feel wounded. Around the centre in a circle, all kinds of pain about yourself.

In the front, above the middle: To feel that you are not able to love. To feel that you lack the joy of life.

In front, just below the diaphragm: To feel bitter in different variations. Obstacles of energy to the bile bladder represent bitterness of having undertaken work/responsibility without being appreciated for it.

The stomach: To feel bitter that your parents or your partner have let you down. This might be memories related to earlier lives that come to the surface because of situations that trigger the memory.

The lungs: To pity oneself in many variations.

At the back, above the middle: At the top, behind the shoulder blades all kinds of longing are situated and then there is frustration, annoyance and irritation.

In the middle of the heart area, at the back: To feel anger. At a circle around the centre; to feel that you are angry with yourself.

At the back below the middle: To feel contempt and self-contempt in a circle around it. Further down, to feel hatred; self-hatred in a circle around it.

The arms and hands belong to the heart area: All kinds of feelings when we have let down others and feelings that others have let us down. A feeling of having let down ourselves lies in the upper arms, further down, when we feel that we have let down others and our family. In the fingers, our children. A feeling of having let down yourself may also give pain in the thumb.

Solar plexus/the belly/the back

The belly: To feel that you are afraid and anxious in many variations. Nervousness and stress (afraid that you are not able to make something in time or the way you have promised). To feel lonely. To feel that you are unfairly treated.

The back: To feel worry and anxiety, to feel fear not to be inadequate. To feel that you have lost your power.

Lower back: To feel that you don't manage to provide what is required for living – an economical worry.

The hip area

Below waist, back: To feel that the others are to blame. To feel that your parents should have done things differently.

The muscles that hold together pelvis and sacrum: Many variations of guilt and guilty conscience.

The muscles in the hip joint: To feel that you are not good enough and to feel that others are better, inferiority in many variations. To feel that you don't know how.

The urinary bladder: To feel that you haven't got enough. To feel that you need much more than you need. Leads to hoarding and greed.

The genitals: To feel that you aren't sufficient sexually. To feel that you aren't sufficient in your partnership.

The thighs

The groin/the upper thighs: To feel that you just want to die or that you are afraid of dying. To feel that you don't want to live or that you only want to go home, is situated at the upper parts of the thighs.

Then pain downwards in the thigh in this order: To feel that you have failed. To feel hopelessness, to feel powerlessness. The middle of the thigh; to feel that you want to give up.

Lower part of the thigh: To feel shame, to feel embarrassed, towards the knee; to feel despair.

The knees and the feet

In the knees: Pain occurs when you face basic choices where the mind cannot understand what the soul wants.

Pain in the legs represents lack of will.

The feet: To feel that there is no point in living. There is pain in the big toe when you feel that you must do something against your will.

Remember that the feelings causing pain usually are at a subconscious level for you. You might not feel such feelings in your daily life even if you have physical pain. You might have felt this way for a memory that happened a long time ago and that made subconscious thoughts start to repeat, which led to pain in the body.

An example showing how pain can occur

A man came to me after a lecture to tell me that the list of emotional pain could not be right. He had so much pain in his feet that he had to walk with sticks, but still he had a great appetite for life. I told him that the thoughts that are creating pain can be totally subconscious so that he needed to sit or lie down and relax and be honest in relation to old memories to find out about it.

It turned out to be a childhood memory where he faced a dilemma. He had to choose between his mother's and his father's way of doing a certain thing. Up through his life he always felt, that if he did it the way his mother meant was best, he let down his father. But if he did what he knew his father would approve of, his mother would be angry. He had lived in a continuing emotional 'roundel' related to his parents through his entire life.

It was time to stop, to take a look at his childhood memories and what the conflict had created up through his life, so that he could release his feelings and free himself from the pain.

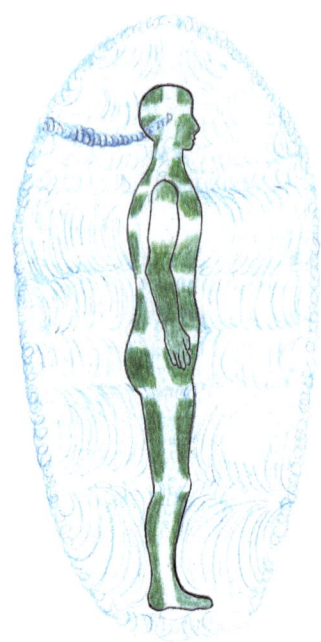

The body's energy field in flow, side view

The picture shows how the different energy channels vibrate (actually communicate) through and around the body. The energy starts from the middle of the chest where the soul is centered. The vibration propagates spiraling forward and backward in a clockwise direction from the heart area. The vibration separates into the entire field. The vibration also propagates upwards and downwards in the same way along the spine and out into the field above and below the body. From the field, the vibration moves back towards the body in channels, still in spiral form. Inside the body the energy propagates to all the cells. The cells are directly connected to the meridian system* that vibrates the energy on and back to the heart/chest area.

The spiral you see at the picture, going from the energy field into the back of the head is a direct connection to the mind – it is the intuition. It gives information to the mind from all the particles in the field.

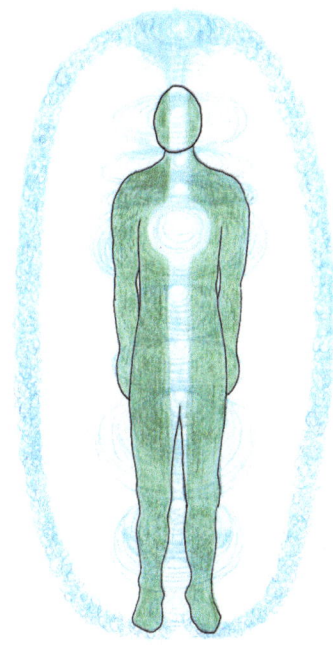

The body's energy field in flow, front view

This sketch shows approximately how the spiral fields lie related to the front of the body. It is equivalent at the back. The channels spiral in straight lines through the body. Via this system the soul's thoughts and feelings are connected to every cell.

If you lie down, another human being can measure the energy in these spiral fields with a pendulum. Then, seen from the other person, the spiral movements are counter-clockwise in the heart channel and clockwise in all the other channel areas. In other words opposite of how it is described from the inside of the body.

8 What makes life work against us?

Let's say you have a friend who annoys you because you feel that he always talks about something he has done when you have told him something you have accomplished. This friend has feelings that make him do just that. Perhaps he has the need to be seen and heard? Maybe he gets eager and wants to share something similar that he starts thinking of whilst you are talking. What you might not be aware of is that the annoyance is just as much about you as about him or you would not have been irritated. There is something about the situation that activates a memory within you. The annoyance is yours, not his. It is likely that you react with annoyance because your friend reminds you about a similar occurrence that made you angry a long time ago. The memory makes your soul remember the irritated feelings you experienced then.

You can choose to regard such situations as opportunities to see what hides in your subconscious by being totally true about your feelings when you are alone. They say exactly what you need to look at in yourself. Try the following: Sit down and imagine what you may feel in the example situation with your friend. What is actually making you irritated? Try out your feelings with these sentences:

I feel that I am annoyed because he always wants to show himself.

I feel that he is stupid because he wants to show himself.

I feel that he wants to be better than me.

I feel annoyed because he never lets me be proud of who I am.

I feel that he always needs to be better than me to show himself to people who are present.

I feel annoyed because I feel that I am not seen when I am with him.

I feel that I am never good enough as the one I am.

I feel that he thinks that he is not worth anything unless he makes things in his own way.

I feel that I am not worth anything unless I get the last word.

I feel that I am not worth much unless I am regarded as the best.

Usually, it's very powerful to feel exactly what you actually feel. Maybe none of these sentences hit you, but still I know that they shed light upon the imaginary situation. If we just try out sentences by guessing, we may suddenly know what it's about. Then your mind has helped your soul to find out about the feelings in the memory that created the annoyance. You notice it immediately when a sentence hits your feelings. If you repeat the sentence, you may feel more feelings coming up. When that happens, you get insights in yourself about what it's about. What is interesting is that you get a much better understanding of your friend and also about the psychological mechanisms inside you. Don't stop if a sentence hits home! The first sentence works as a door opener into many feelings from the same and similar memories. Usually there are many feelings you need to put into words. Search for more triggered feelings and say them loud to yourself until you are empty and realise that you understand the entire situation.

I hope the imaginary situation above may shed light upon what I want to explain so that you can transfer it to your own life. This is one of the patterns/trigger-situations I have discovered as archetypical*. When you have worked through such situations and released the pain, using the method described in this book, you will no longer be annoyed, for example when your friend tells something to surprise you… You feel generous and let him be the way he is. His way of behavior might even be gone! Perhaps it was your pattern first? Maybe he didn't have the need to be seen at all... maybe it was your interpretation of the situation based on your wounds and repeated thoughts, that made it repeat itself? Because this is the way the smaller and larger conflicts inside and outside of us occur.

To start with the patterns we carry along with us are difficult to set eyes on because they simply characterise our personality...we think it is the way we are! We push away unpleasant feelings like we always have done. It may make us think and act the opposite of what we feel, like in the case with the friend, who you feel put himself forward. – Because if so, he does it because he feels small and has the need to be seen and heard. Maybe he was scolded once as a boy when had done something he was proud about?

Our human nature is to want to feel good, so we have the tendency to push away the painful feelings when unpleasant situations occur. We try to pull ourselves together and do our best. Often we try to continue as if nothing has happened. The feelings we push away, however, don't leave us for that reason. We only push them into the subconscious where they are creating our emotional reactions. The soul has less ability to logic reasoning than the mind. It might make the pain that is experienced in painful situations become the truth for the person. For example, the wounded soul concludes by saying: 'I am not being seen. Everybody leaves me'. Or 'The others are so stupid'. Exactly what the soul feels is then repeated in the subconscious and sent out to the surroundings as creating energy so that similar episodes occur.

This is why it is important to understand that particles communicate with each other. I have found that the particles in a person's energy field tell us what the person's subconscious repeats in his /her cells. Thoughts that are repeated function as creating energy, actually as a kind of programming, and make the particles surrounding the person try to fulfill the repeating sentences. Both humans and animals will try to fulfill what is repeated. Even technical devices that we use, for example your car, get influenced by repeating thoughts at the particle level. Do you say a sentence loud to yourself when things turn bad for you? Try to notice what turns faulty for you!

Maybe you think this sounds strange, but I think that humans will start observing life and find out about such phenomena. We will stop saying that 'there is much between heaven and earth that we don't understand…' We will rather study what is happening around us in new ways. If you have the intention of managing something and don't make it, the particles might have listened to the subconscious instead of your conscious thoughts.

Here is an example about how a wound from adolescence created repeating situations

A friend exclaimed one day, rather irritated: 'You don't listen when I speak to you! This is the way it was with my husband too, he often ignored me and might suddenly walk out of the room while I was talking'! I had to admit that it was true… often my thoughts wandered and it was difficult to concentrate about what she said. The particular time when this happened, I actually listened, but I was simultaneously busy searching for something and went into another room and she interpreted my lack of attention as if I ignored her. What is interesting to look at in this case, is what she said: 'You don't listen when I speak'. This was exactly what her subconscious mind repeated! As she immediately added that her husband had overheard her, this was obviously a repeating pattern, created by a situation where she was not listened to. As she was an eager practitioner of the Keys of Liberation, she realised it right away and searched to try to find the memory that created the pattern.

She went back to her childhood, and quite promptly a memory from the age of 12 showed up. She had been playing with peers, boys and girls in a plank cabin and they had dressed up putting on some lipstick that they had got hold of. When she came home and had excitedly told her parents how fun this had been, her parents didn't want to listen.

They were religious and as you can imagine what she had been into worried them, both relating to their beliefs and to the responsibility they felt about her awakening sexuality. Her father left the room while she was talking. She felt that he turned his back on her. This created a painful memory and a pattern saying that when she was talking about something of importance for her, she was not listened to. I performed the pattern's 'order' literary speaking, because I left the room while she was talking. It had created similar situations until on that day she wanted to release it by the help of the Keys of liberation. People around her 'obeyed' exactly what her inner child was sending out. The energy in her field sent out signals about how she was not listened to and my subconscious responded by not giving attention.

When we are in situations that remind us about what happened, the pain is repeated. This way unexpected situations are created, which make similar things happen to out of what created the wound in the first place. Suddenly your car doesn't want to move just when you are very busy. And when you reflect on it, this has happened before… is it because you say out loud your annoyance when it happens?

When pain is repeated in the soul and thus in the cells, new painful situations are created, because the particles' nature is to create what is told to them repeatedly. The souls of persons around us then respond, repeating statements and thus new situations that resemble it occur. Thus new wounds may occur and be repeated.

Eventually as life goes on and we continue to suppress our feelings, chronical pain and disease are the results. Souls may not only repeat when something hurts. They may also enhance and multiply to manage when feeling that something is difficult. It is very usual and happens when a person is engaged. However, when there is an emotional pain being repeated and the soul enhances to make it through the day, the emotional pain really gets worse. So if you have physical pain, the first thing you need to do, is to speak directly to your soul: 'Please, my soul, stop enhancing, stop multiplying'! The pain may go away or at least become weaker. If it really works, go on telling your soul the logic of not enhancing pain!

Our lives are woven into each other for better or worse. It is advantageous to dissolve that which doesn't benefit us so that we can feel good about ourselves and each other. The feelings triggered in our daily lives are our 'indicator lamps' that tell us about what is hidden in us. To set us completely free, we need to realise that it is not enough superficially to feel what happens. Usually we need to go back to the memory and feel the difficult feelings to make our soul understand that it isn't the way we subconsciously concluded at the time when it happened.

In most cultures we have learned to pull ourselves together, not to cry but to rather push away emotions. Some people get embarrassed and tell those who cry to stop crying. I think it's time to change the culture of what is accepted and is natural for us. It is actually essential to allow oneself to cry because what is suppressed inside of the single human being, is what makes humans get ill. It is also what makes humans blame, criticise and create conflicts. It's the pain we carry that makes us avoid someone or something. It may even make us dishonest – which again leads to unacceptable behavior. Ultimately, to allow ourselves and each other to cry is necessary to create peace in the world! What we need to be happy with ourselves and each other, is to learn to leave behind and let go of painful situations.

What I recommend, is to work through the feelings as they show up in your daily life. They influence our lives much more than humans are aware of. There are many reasons to take seriously what we carry in our psyche. Situations that create sentences like, 'It was my fault, I couldn't help it', 'I am always the one who is the last in the line' or 'I am always the one left standing alone', may have happened in everyday life. As a child or teenager at the time, we might have looked smiling a while after the situation was over, it was because we were told not to cry. It isn't necessarily incapable parents or traumatic situations that created the sentences. Nevertheless, they may result in exactly what they say; someone is blamed for something seriously bad, which they haven't done because they as children might have made a mistake that they regretted and are repeating subconsciously. Others may be pushed out and not allowed to be part of a community because they repeat an excluding sentence that constantly gets stronger, unless the pattern is broken and the person manages to set him or herself free.

We might even contribute to creating abuse situations for ourselves by our own unfortunate thought patterns, especially if they are reinforced by several similar situations. As we see; to learn to understand how the psyche influences what is happening between people is important for all parts of society. This information will give new knowledge to initiatives to prevent bullying both at school and in working places. I hope this book will shed light upon such and similar conditions.

In the 90s several books about affirmations* were published. An affirmation means to repeat confirming statements to achieve what you want in life. In addition they told us to visualise what you want to achieve. There was a conviction that repeating thoughts are creating and that positive thoughts can manifest what we imagine. It felt right. Still, I never managed to achieve what I wished for in spite of doing my best to believe in what I repeated. I even sang positive sentences to achieve success. Later I found the reason. It was because I at that time carried many wounds and limiting thoughts in my subconscious. This worked against what I wished for in life. I discovered that if you have wounds in your soul so that you have subconscious belief patterns that say the opposite of what you wish for, the positive affirmations will push the negative thoughts up to the surface of the mind!

It may feel painful to learn the information about these phenomena that I have found in our psyche, but actually, you can choose to turn it on its head and see it positively. Now you can figuratively choose to get started with a porch, pick and shovel and work to find what you until now haven't seen in your inner landscape! See the obstacles as challenges and grow day by day. If you look at tears as something painful, or you think what I write is negative, it might be a heavy job. But if you choose to think that tears lead to release, insights in yourself and joy, you will experience a constantly richer and more exciting life.

The way that has turned out to be the most useful for putting behind negative thoughts for me, is to realise whatever I feel that hurts. *The reason that acknowledgment of feelings really works, is that we can only let go of what we are willing to realise that we feel.*

9 A new approach

'Why do I need to realise what hurts', many people say. It is extremely important to underline that you shall not acknowledge the situation that made you feel what you felt. You need to realise what you *feel* so that you can set yourself free from feelings that don't serve you. We shall neither accept offence nor betrayal, but make it clear that we reject bad behavior. Nevertheless, painful feelings may occur even if the person who caused them didn't mean to hurt us.

It is very important to realise that the feelings are our own, whoever causes them. It means that we don't need to express our feelings to those that cause them, unless it's natural and important then and there. If we have emotional reactions that are much stronger than expected in a situation, we can be fairly sure that a memory that triggered the reaction and then it is best to bring your feelings to a place where you can be alone. The usual pattern is to blame the situation or the people that caused the feelings. But people cannot dissolve what is stuck inside of you when you feel pain! Only you can. You are the only person who can work through your feelings.

We can choose to see the situations that trigger strong feelings as gold mines in our lives. Instead of being angry with people, or afraid and in despair when we are having difficulties, we can work through the feelings in ways that make us able to put behind what is difficult. There are ways out of both fear and despair. By stopping and realising exactly what you feel when you are on your own, instead of expressing it to the person involved, you might find the aggression and the need to blame leaves you rather quickly. You will get clarity about exactly what you feel and you will achieve insights as well. Having said that…anger, despair and all the feelings that may show up, don't need to have their roots in the past. They may be caused by someone or something happening here and now. Still, I recommend you work through the feelings about what happened when you have got a distance to it. It will give you insights and the possibility to forgive both yourself and others.

Realising sentences may be used directly in daily situations that you experience as difficult, so that you handle your life in a better way. When you start to realise what you feel, you get clarity into what you feel so that you can see what it's about. It is also a very fine way to get connected to your soul. Although situations usually show you something that has happened earlier, working through your feelings as soon as you are on your own can be a good training in using the Keys of Liberation.

An example of use of realising sentences to achieve clarity

A friend used the keys when she came home after an episode when she was jealous at ladies that were attending the training studio where her boyfriend was working.
I realise that I am jealous when my boyfriend talks to that lady who is in love with him.
I realise that I am sorry that he didn't ask me to come up to them to present myself.
I realise that I feel wounded when he doesn't relate to me as soon I drop by the studio.
She realised this and made positive realising sentences to make an agreement with herself to manage the situations in the studio in a better way:
I realise that it is a part of his job to talk with women.
I realise that he has every right to talk to whoever he wants without me getting jealous.
She got clarity so that she could see and understand what made her angry with him… and she realised that it was all about herself.

10 The Keys of Liberation

Key number 1
Realising what we actually feel

I had strived to love myself for many years when I came across a book where it mentioned that accepting oneself was important to achieve a happy life. I discovered that I had to accept myself the way I was, with all those complexes and tendencies I had. Then something important happened! The limitations started to dissolve. It doesn't work to wait until you have lost weight or until you have stopped smoking! We have bad habits and comfort mechanisms because of emotional wounds. To take care of ourselves, we need to realise that things are the way they are. Then the body responds. To dare to admit your weaknesses actually leads to getting to know yourself. Pretending to be something we are not, works against its purpose because then we create more limitations in the energy system. The more honest we are in relation to ourselves, the better it is. By being totally honest you are able to release a lot because there might be shame and avoidance strategies that make you unable to understand what to do. To be honest with oneself is about acceptance and acknowledgement.

To start with, realising what you feel seems like a paradox for many people. To realise what you always have tried to push away may seem wrong until you understand these mechanisms. The feelings coming up when you start realising are often not what you expected. Suddenly you sit and cry because of a grief of someone who left you in your youth when you thought it was about annoyance concerning your husband. Or you discover when you move your thought into the neck pain that you as a 4 year old weren't visible for mum the day she started to go to work. You felt that she didn't see you anymore, but always left you and was busy with her own things at the time when you used to sit and cuddle.

When we start realising exactly what we feel, something 'magical' often happens. More feelings come up to the surface and we understand more of what it is about. We may get glimpses of memories and suddenly we see exactly what we need to go back to childhood or youth about. The more we manage to express exactly what we feel about a memory whilst being in it, the better it is. We need to be totally honest with ourselves. Suddenly the pain can dissolve and be gone. In the cases when it happens whilst realising what you feel, your soul releases at the soul level. Usually you get insights into why you reacted the way you did, and you understand that it doesn't serve you to go around carrying such feelings, so you manage to let go of them. You need to say aloud exactly what you feel and *do the best you can to say why you feel that way.*

The template for the realizing sentences is as in this example:

'I realise that I feel *that I made a fool of myself'*

You need to be alone so that other people's presence doesn't prevent you from bringing out the feelings... Sometimes you need to allow yourself to shout loud if you need it! When you start realising what you feel, you may experience that your body starts moving. It might jump and you might feel tickling in the muscles. This happens because your soul is present in you and may start spinning the particles you consist of. Sometimes the physical pain might move. It's because different cells within an area contain different aspects of the same issue you are working on.

Humans may be completely blocked in the heart area. If so, they have little ability to love and may have difficulties understanding such feelings that emanate from the heart; compassion, care, joy by community and affection, and similar, but are in the understanding of the mind. Then grief, anger, despair and the feeling of betrayal etc. might block the heart energy so that the person is not able to cry. Some people have experienced shock. It means that their soul could not take in the total truth, but ran away. When this is the case, the wounds are so deep that it is as if a physical lid covers the heart area. Still… when the person starts realising pain based on his or her logic understanding about what the mind knows, it starts dissolving. If the person manages to feel a tiny bit of a true feeling, it's like winding up a thread. The more the person who has pain is able to put his or her feelings into words, the better it works. The tears might not be there to start with, but when they come, it might be like a waterfall.

The challenge about this is to get inside the feelings. In such cases it helps to visualise and feel that there is a lid above the chest and then imagine that you take it away, as if it is physical. Another way may be to combine logic with the list of where in the body the different types of feelings are stored. If you have physical pain, it may help you to get started. Perhaps the blockage is felt like a knife in the heart or like a big stone. To visualise yourself lifting it might make you able to start opening up to the heart feelings. The technique 'The inner child' further back in the book might also be of great help. When we see ourselves from the outside, our ability to care helps us get into the feelings.

Key number 2
Forgiving the feelings

Most of us learnt in our childhood that it is important to forgive those who hurt us. I also learnt to ask for forgiveness when I felt that I had done something wrong. I learnt it from good teachers in primary school. These basic ways of relating to each other are really important to keep running if we want to stay healthy and create a better world for all. I miss this topic in public debate. Perhaps many painful conflicts could have been left behind by many people who suffer, if forgiveness and reconciliation at a personal level is applied as a tool in politics and conflict solving? Maybe it's time to bring forgiveness forth to see ourselves and each other in a new light? Maybe forgiveness could be a topic in school? It is always important to be able to leave behind painful situations. The condition is that we know what forgiveness means and that we mean it when we forgive someone. We all need to learn it from childhood. I wonder if it is practiced in homes?

It is only you who are carrying what is painful for you. The person you have a grudge with, are bitter or angry at, might not know. It depends on her or his experience of what happened. Maybe the person feels guilt or shame without being willing to admit it? Perhaps those emotions are the reason the person is arrogant and blames others? The pain that lies inside us may cause many projections and actions of less character related to others.

One of the most important things I have discovered *is to forgive ourselves* for things we have done that we feel bad about. Related to a key process, it is always necessary to take a look at whether you feel that you did something stupid. To begin with, such recognition might be difficult, but as you discover how wonderful it is to let go of what you regret that you did, I am sure you start forgiving very willingly.

In addition, the second key contains *an important element that is different from other release methods*. I discovered that it is important to forgive oneself for painful feelings. To forgive that you have felt something else than good feelings, which is the nature of the soul. It proved to be very useful to be able to leave behind painful memories completely. You can choose to work systematically and say out loud that you forgive yourself for all the feelings that came up during the first key, for example:

'*I forgive myself that I feel* for making a fool of myself'.

The reason it is important to forgive oneself for having felt painful feelings, is that the energy we consist of is love, so what we actually do, is to forgive ourselves for feeling something else than love and joy.

When you use this key, you can choose to see yourself outside of yourself. (See also the chapter The inner child) You can for example speak to yourself and say:

'I forgive you, «Your name», that you feel that you have made a fool of yourself'.

Then you function as a caregiver for a part of your soul. This is a very effective way to work. Often you may get up more feelings and start crying. Then I recommend that you realise what you feel as 'I' before you continue.

During the forgiveness work, it's important to feel who you need to forgive. It may often be caring people who we feel have failed, even if they didn't understand how we felt. There may also be things that are really hard to forgive when you look back at it. Remember then, that all people, including our parents have their own baggage of painful feelings when they respond and act.

We cannot always understand how adults could have done what they have done to children, but still it is important to find a perspective for what happened, so that we are able to forgive. It is an important part of the healing process. When it comes to our parents, it's beneficial to know their childhood, upbringing and adult life. It makes it easier to see extenuating circumstances. It really eases the pressure to ask for forgiveness and even more if we hug the people we relate to! But if you think it is difficult related to heavy situations that happened back in time, you may reach them at the soul level by speaking to them frankly from your heart. That is the fine thing with working this way. What happens then is that the climate between you and the person you relate to becomes much better, and maybe you manage to bring up the issue that was difficult between you – simply because you don't carry the pain anymore.

You can do this any time. Feel if you need to ask anyone for forgiveness. You can sit down with closed eyes and visualise that the person sits in front of you. When you really mean it, you dissolve the pain inside of you. If you do this truthfully, you reach their soul which exists through time and space. You will know it when they have forgiven you. You may see by your inner eye that they nod and get happy. This works even with people who are dead and are in another dimension. What is important, is that you mean what you say from your heart.

When you work through forgiveness, remember that you carry thought patterns that may have roots far back in time and that are creating energy in your subconscious that may make situations in your life occur. This perspective may be so new to you that you need time to accept that it is this way? I see it as important to realise that it is this way because we always so easily put blame on others when life goes against us. Many people object to start with when I claim that painful situations can be created by themselves but when they start to realise it, it doesn't take long until the feelings that come up, say the same.

Realise that all humans are on a journey through life and that you don't know what others have in their emotional baggage. Everybody is at different phases in their development. It is as we are in a huge school with pupils at all levels. For example, some are in the first grade and some in the graduating class. We would not look down at a pupil in the first grade, would we? Neither would we think about the pupils in the graduating class that they are more valuable as people? If you bitterly regret something you did… or there are things you said or did without thinking, don't be too hard on yourself! It is usually the emotional baggage that makes us do things we regret. You find the way when you are honest and find extenuating circumstances.

Key number 3
Love for oneself

It is said that one needs to love oneself to be able to love others. Now I have realied that it is difficult for other people to love me if I have many self-criticising thoughts. It was the wish to learn to love myself that led me to develop this method. It was because I discovered that self-critical thoughts prevented me from accepting myself the way I am.

When you forgive, the wound starts to heal. Actively say to yourself that you love yourself, heal your soul and restore the life energy in your cells. It makes you bloom! Every single particle responds to the love you give yourself. Often forgiveness and love merge into each other and we need to give ourselves love before we can work with forgiveness. Make the situation as real as possible and give comfort, understanding and love. Talk with yourself in the present! Then you experience fully being present with yourself at the time you were in trouble. You are the one that knows you the best. Your soul knows exactly what you need. Simultaneously you need to be aware of how several patterns get to the surface because your soul longs to be happy and loved.

For you who feel alone or who aren't happy in your relationship; you don't need to go around waiting for someone to love you. Eventually, as you learn to love yourself as the one you are, the longing for confirmation dissolves. The Keys, the way I present them here, imply that you feel more and more love for yourself every time you work through a memory. Gradually you get much more chance to be happy in a relationship because you don't need others to confirm you. You will find peace with yourself rather than crave for someone outside of you to see you and love you. It doesn't work to use this technique without looking at what is preventing you from loving yourself.

So how come many people repeat on a subconscious level that they are not worthy of being loved? I have discovered that this is one of the archetypical patterns that most people carry around. It is a pattern that make us long for confirmation – and which makes many marriages unravel. It is activated in most people when we as small children start feeling that we have done something wrong.

An everyday example

The little child that you were maybe experienced doing something funny and exciting in your eyes. For example when you made mud cakes and very happily came trudging into the living room to let dad "taste"…But instead of "pretending-tasting" he laughed at you and pulled you outdoors to let go of the mud cake whilst you screamed because you felt that you weren't respected for being the beautiful, creative child that you were. Then just as bewildered, you were taken to the bathroom and washed in the face and your hands in a way that you felt was an assault. After the happening you felt like a crater inside and you became totally silent until you were led to do something that made you forget, watch television, for example. Your soul may have concluded that you had no value in your father's eyes. That he knew everything much better that you. That you were stupid and not worthy of being loved… because your father didn't have the ability to show you love and comfort in the situation. The reason he wasn't able to comfort might have been that he never had been comforted as a child. He probably wasn't connected to his inner child, so he had forgotten how fun it is to pretend that you are big and able to make a cake like the adults do? He didn't feel that he was bad to you… rather the contrary. He probably meant he was a good father.

I do not mean to make life difficult for parents. Rather the contrary. When you realise how little it takes before the child is upset, you as a parent will handle situations with greater care. What is particularly important, is to give attention when children are proud of themselves and about things they have made or done.

This is a need that all people have and it is essential for the development of self-esteem. (See also the chapter Parents and children)

The situation that is described above is the basis for creating what I call a Gordian knot* in our inner being. The creative child feels that its proud, positive experience leads to it being ignored and experiencing feeling ridiculed and humiliated. As an adult, the person cannot understand why painful things happen in their life when they only are positive and creative. However, if the pattern is saying: 'When I am creating and want to show what I have made, I am offended by he who I love the most'. Then it might happen later in life too.

When we release such and similar wounds, it is important that we take time to appreciate ourselves as a part of the process. From the very start I neatly have made all the realising sentences into love sentences. In this way I work consistently through every feeling. These are templates for love phrases:

'I love you, "Your name" even if you feel that you made a fool of yourself'.

This is natural to do in the continuing work when you use the forgiveness key in a similar manner, speaking to yourself as if you are outside of you.

If you choose to say it to yourself:

'I love myself, even if I feel that I made a fool of myself'.

What is important to notice, is that we say 'even if'. There is forgiveness in those words that works in the same way as the life energy's function in the body. It is the love inside of you as long as you live.

Love for oneself from a limited perspective may become selfishness. But if you choose to look into your life, you are not selfish.

True love for yourself has nothing to do with greed, jealousy or seeking attention. Selfishness is fear of not being loved, not having enough, for being neglected or rejected. I guess many of us have been selfish when we were afraid of not getting our share… True love for ourselves means that we accept the way we look and dress so that our body feels well. Then we radiate our inner qualities as well.

Key number 4
To let go means to leave behind

Sometimes it is enough to realise what you feel and then forgive and the painful feelings dissolve when the soul realises that it doesn't serve to carry the pain. Nevertheless, it is important to look back and really feel if the painful feelings are gone. We need to be willing to leave things behind. Sometimes we need to take an active decision to let go of the feelings and thoughts about a situation. If you still feel painful feelings, there is more to realise and forgive. Or maybe another memory that created similar feelings is waiting to be released?

You will feel good by working thoroughly through the let-go-sentences. Say them loud to yourself when applying this key. To work consistently to let go of all the emotions in all sentences that had triggered your feelings by the first key, make you aware of what you have achieved. There is no doubt that it is the most efficient and profound. It is what gives the most insights also. Suddenly you realise that: 'I have always believed this about myself, as if it was the truth! Now I see that is doesn't serve to walk around thinking this way!' Such insights lead to enormous joy, spreading in the body.

When you look back at your life, there may be things you have experienced that you don't want to leave behind. What happened was just too painful. What was done was just too awful. I do understand that. Still I ask you to ask yourself this question: Do I want to go on carrying hatred, bitterness and pain in my subconscious? In my body? Because it is the way it works. It is *you* who get sick if you don't let go of the bad feelings. I say this because the person who has done bad things to you or someone you love or loved, might not have the ability or willingness to ask for forgiveness in an unforeseeable future. Maybe you can forgive yourself for the hatred and the bitterness? It will ease the pressure inside. I do not mean to say that we shall accept humans' evil acts. Absolutely not. However, we need to learn to leave behind painful things to be able to go on after awful misdeeds. We shall always say stop when we are offended or betrayed. We need to tell out loud what we mean, as best we can. I mean that we need to realise that we must live on after bad accidents and awful acts of violence. The best way I have found, is to realise what I feel, cry out the pain and receive the insights this gives. It will give you a tremendous strength instead of repeating the pain inside. However, it is necessary to get a distance to very painful things that have happened in your life before you start using the keys to leave it behind. The key sounds like this:

'*I now let go that I feel* that I made a fool of myself'.

If something inside of you still feels unpleasant, you need to go back to forgiveness or realising feelings to find out what it is. When you have finished a release work like this, you feel peacefulness in body and soul. You need to lie down and relax and enjoy how your body responds to the work by rejoicing. Feel the joy and satisfaction. Sometimes you sense that the blood flows to areas that have been blocked, other times you will sense tingling.

When you reflect on the release work, you constantly get new insights in your own life and thus in life in general. It gives great joy. It is important for me to underline this because I have been criticised for focusing on negative things. It is not what I do. I show that we cannot be peaceful inside unless we know what prevents us from being so. It is not possible to push negative thoughts away only by focusing on the positive. To discover these mechanisms makes us grow day by day when we choose to use this method. I experience it as groundbreaking and exciting. For many years we have learned to think positively to achieve good lives. Of course we need to! This is a technique that you bring forth when you want to look at unpleasant things.

I don't think humanity has any other choice than to learn to understand our own nature and act upon it.

11 The inner child

When we look back at childhood memories, we may experience being there as if it was yesterday and the feelings are just as strong. The inner child is an important part of our soul. During my development, I read John Bradshaw*'s book 'Homecoming' with the subtitle: 'Reclaiming and healing your inner child'. It became a door opener for me. Lately I have understood how the inner child actually is a part of our soul, especially when we have dissolved the memories from childhood and youth that hurts. You will always be playful and creative when you allow yourself to be this part of you. To be childlike is a gift. The inner child in you finds the life joy and gives your life perspectives you had forgotten when you allow yourself to let go of inhibitions. The inner child has its own wisdom about the soul's deepest secrets. As you work with your inner child, you will experience great growth and self-knowledge.

At the time I was a teacher in an elementary school, I experienced having 6 year old pupils in gymnastics. 6 year old children are happy simply by coming into a gymnastic hall, it seems. They immediately start running and shouting, rejoicing from being able to unfold freely in such a huge space. The child's ability to rejoice by existence lives inside of us! I am optimistic about the future and I am so because I know that our inner children carry a great wisdom that will start activating the world's population in new ways as we release the baggage from our childhood.

You can start releasing your inner child at any time, even if you have neither things that bother you nor grief for anything. You can find exciting things about yourself and develop yourself in a new way. And you can prevent your patterns from getting stronger as you grow older. For example, you can browse in old pictures or you can see old relatives that make you think backwards in time. For instance, sit down and think of where you lived the day you started to go to school. Imagine that you are there as the one you were at that time. This is like traveling back in time and a great exercise in finding situations that you can look at. Suddenly you remember something of importance!

If you are having a hard time and life seems to work against you, I recommend you work through your feelings daily until it lightens. And it may do so quite soon! Very often it is situations from your childhood that show up first. Then you will actually want to work on them because you see that releasing a memory works so positively. Take a look at the methods of how to find the memories and go ahead. Maybe a memory has shown up while you read this?

When you work with your inner child, please remember that you were a child at that time. As a child you need time and care. When you have finished realising what you feel in a situation, I recommend that you imagine that you move into the picture/memory as the adult person you are today. See yourself as a caregiver for the child you were then. Keep your eyes shut so that your imagination is the tool that keeps you in the memory. Clear away others who are present so that you are alone with yourself. Then, find a position where you win trust. Talk with your child, sit down for instance on the floor (in your imagination) and ask if he/she wants to come and sit on your lap. Or you can create a bench or a chair in your imagination. Make it comfortable so that you can imagine the both of you sitting like this for a long time. The situation you create in your thoughts is really real for your soul. I generally have a big cushion at my disposal. I imagine that the cushion is the child I give comfort, so that I hold my arms around myself.

It might take time until the child wants to sit on the lap. Sometimes she/he might be so hurt that she/he doesn't want to listen to anyone, not even you. She/he may also have so much feeling of guilt and shame that she/he doesn't want to believe in you. You need to use all the love and patience you have in your heart to make your inner child listen to you. Tell her that you love her/him, even if she/he did what she/he did. Tell her that she is actually made of love. – That everybody can make mistakes. Forgive her/him for what she/he feels is wrong. Repeat and repeat.

Rock her/him in your arms. When you do this, the wound starts to heal. You heal yourself with love. You are actually relating to yourself as if you are an extra parent at the time it happened but who knows what's going to happen through your life. You can say: 'I am the one you will be when you grow up. May I be your extra-mom (dad)? '

Very often, what happens is that this caring kind of situation really makes the feelings come up. Then the tears come. Then you need to go back to realising feelings again. Again put all feelings into words…this may be many sentences. Your compassion with yourself usually triggers an emotional avalanche. In this way we can switch between positions and roles within. We then achieve finding comfort and strengthened love for ourselves. Very painful memories demand that we move back and forth between positions several times and take breaks in between.

To forgive those that hurt you, you need to be in the position of the child in the forgiveness phase. I have experienced clients saying that they are certain that they have no unsettled issues related to their parents. Still, when they move back and experience being themselves as children in a situation, they may still be angry with their parents and have the need to forgive them. Some may have thought that they have forgiven their parents for episodes that happened a long time ago but then during key-work when they travel back they may discover that they have put a lid on the feelings…which create subconscious ways of relating to other people. When you have worked through a caring conversation where you forgive all the painful feelings, you need to do something important. You need to imagine that the person you were then belongs in your heart, meaning in the middle of the chest. You need to do this because the part of your soul that you have related to, needs to be together with the rest of the soul with his or her new insights. Keep your eyes tight shut and imagine that you look into your inner child's eyes and ask if she/he is OK. Ask: 'Do you want to live in my heart?' If you get no, there is more about the memory you need to look at together. If she/he says yes, you can imagine that the two of you create a room in the heart where she/he will enjoy being. It may be a room you remember from your childhood, a new room or it can be a place in nature – a place that you enjoyed as a child. The idea often comes spontaneously from the child. Use time for this and when the child in your imagination has found a place to play and enjoy her/himself, ask the child if you can go on. If she/he answers yes, you can continue and know that you have left the difficult memory behind. Then you can feel the tranquility and joy by having integrated new insights.

It is very important that the child finds its place in the heart when you have finished. Your soul consists of many components and all of them must know that they belong to you, that they are you. Or the part of your soul that you have worked with might find another place to stay, for example in another person where it feels more secure. Every childhood memory that isn't worked through represents a part of you that expresses its pain. When we work like this, we become whole little by little. Many people have a kind of 'black hole' inside that represents their longing for someone to confirm and love them the way they are. Every time we create space and integrate the child in the heart, we reduce the black hole by loving ourselves.

An example of releasing my inner child

An evening many years ago, I felt so discouraged. I wanted to give in. It is strange, I thought, because during the day I had repeated affirmations* about being proud of being myself. During the night I was heavy at heart. I woke up and couldn't sleep… I was not able to change the thoughts to being positive. When I woke up the next morning, I was just as sad. I understood it was caused by a memory that I could find out about. I asked for help by the help of my pendulum*.

I needed to go back to my childhood. By the help of yes- and no-questions to my pendulum, I soon found an experience from the time when I was 6 years old. We had recently moved to a new place. I had got acquainted with a girl of my age in the neighborhood. It was early autumn and outside their house her big brother had got the task of throwing firewood in through a basement window. He must have been about 11 or 12 years old. He wanted us small girls to work with him. He told us not to dislodge the stick of wood that kept the window open, or else… (I remember he used some very rude expressions.) As the window was turning inwards and I could not see it, I didn't understand what he meant. I found the job very joyful and eagerly I started to throw. Can you imagine how proud I was when this big boy asked me for help! I felt very proud… and good at it! Until I hit the stick that kept the window open… and bang!

It fell down and the glass broke. Scared to death I ran home, being certain that the boy would beat me. I remember now I was afraid of that boy all the time, as long as we lived at that place. I met him once later and then again he told me he wanted to beat me up. That was the memory.

I went into the feelings when it happened. Suddenly I remembered the pride! I remembered that I was so happy and felt it was so joyful… until the catastrophe happened. It was me! I was the one making the mistake! It was my fault. I had broken a window and there was no one to comfort me, only someone who wanted to punish me. I remember I didn't dare tell my parents about it.

Now I understood why I had been in such a bad temper and had become totally discouraged. I had repeated to myself the entire day yesterday that I was proud to be the one I am. This was about an irrational pattern that had become triggered and pushed up to the surface by the affirmations. In this memory I felt that my pride by being good at what I did, led to misery. I felt that I did a disastrous mistake… and even more, I was threatened by the most awful punishment. This is what I call a Gordian knot* it means a good, positive feeling ending up in a painful result. I used the first key about it in this way:

I realise that I feel that when I am proud about being good at something, I do a mistake and then it's my fault that a catastrophe happens.

I realise that I feel that everything is my fault.

I realise that I feel that when I am proud of being a part of the team, I expect punishment…

I realise that I feel that I deserve punishment when I do my best to help.

I realise that I am afraid that the boy will beat me up.

I tried out many sentences and I tried as best as I could to hit my feelings. I did my best to get the positive intention and the negative outcome in the same sentence. Those that really hurt, I repeated and repeated until the painful feelings started to fade... but still, I wasn't finished.

When I started on the second key, forgiving, I was filled with the painful feelings again and I decided to use the inner child technique. In my imagination I left myself as a child and then entered the picture as my adult self. I squatted to speak to little Inger. She was still terrified by fear! (Something was interesting when I did this... I was really back there when it happened because I heard her voice! She spoke the dialect I spoke until I was 8 years old.) I told her that it was an accident. That I had seen that she was very good at it. I explained everything to her from my adult, calming position. I told her that I liked the fact that she was proud of herself. She did not want to come to me at first, but argued against me. She sobbed and was still convinced that she deserved nothing but punishment! I didn't give in, but said: I love you just the way you are. It doesn't matter if the window is broken. I love you even if you feel you will get punished for being proud when you are good at things. At last I gained her trust so that she was happy to sit on my lap and felt secure. I could hold my arms around her and we worked through the forgiveness. At last she could play in her room in my heart and felt safe and happy. Then I could state to myself that the pain from that memory was behind me.

12 Parents and children

One of the most important things I have learnt by working with myself and others, is to understand how important it is be considerate and to treat all human beings with respect, even small children. It is because emotional wounds that occur in our daily lives are always created by other human beings who are too busy or are angry, who don't understand or who don't have sufficient insight or compassion. The many small choices we do, constantly influence the lives of other humans to a large extent. For instance, when we don't do something we know is right related to our children because we don't have time or because we are too tired or too lazy, it's time to stop and reflect on this. Parents should not let children decide everything. Parents need to set boundaries and explain why they do it and show by being good examples. Then the children appreciate the boundaries because they feel that their parents are attentive and really care about them. Can you agree with this when you look back at your own life?

Here is an example of a client showing how important it is to understand our parents in the light of their own emotional baggage

'The summer I was turning four, our family lived in a hired cabin for a period. One day I had got an idea to help my mother to lay the table. Proudly I had taken the sugar bowl from the kitchen to carry it to the table in the living room. I never got that far. I lost it and it was smashed and the sugar ended up on the floor in glass pieces. I was terribly upset because my Mum and dad were angry with me even though I just wanted to help.

My parents had their patterns of reaction, which made them both annoyed and worried. They had to sort sugar and broken glass. They had rented the cabin including inventory and had to pay for the sugar bowl. What initially was my joyous and helpful action led to their reactions, which created a pattern in me that sounded something like this: 'When I am proud and happy by helping, those that I love get angry with me... and then they don't love me any more'. It showed up to be a Gordian knot* because my soul interpreted the situation so that it was my proud act that made them angry.

When I worked through this episode, many contradictory feelings came up because the little girl that I was interpreted the situation as very painful. My parents could not remember it; to them it was an everyday situation. I forgave them and left it behind me. Later it showed up that this wound in me had its roots in several earlier lives. Because of that, the episode in the cabin activated far more and stronger feelings than what was logical in the situation'.

The ways we react are often related to the ways our parents brought us up and their demands of how we should be when we grew up. The upbringing contributes largely to form us and when we as old souls incarnate in small children, contradictions may occur in the belief system of our soul and the belief system of our parents. Our parents have brought their belief system from their parents. Therefore, to be honest about what we actually feel about our parents is a part of the process of freeing ourselves from emotional reactions. There are episodes in most people's lives when we have been very angry and wounded because of our parents. It doesn't mean that we don't love them! It means exactly what it is; a wound that needs to be healed so that we don't go on having grudges. Most parents do their best as parents. Even when you have a good relationship to your parents as an adult, it is important to look at the episodes from your childhood and youth when you can remember that you felt angry, wounded, abandoned, offended or let down. The memories contribute to form your life and your patterns of reaction. If they are triggered by the people you create loving relations with later in life, you may project anger and painful feelings towards them.

Because of the growing insights I have got in my own life, I see more and more how the best way is to relate to children in their upbringing. This is some of the most positive I have learned by self-development work. When I reached this insight, my own children had grown up, so I could not change what I had done, but I could speak to them about episodes when I remembered, in which I knew I acted wrongly. I have asked for forgiveness. I have told them about situations when I was in despair so that they as adults could understand why I was acting the way I did at the time they were children. It was necessary for me to be totally honest both to them and to myself. When we as adult parents work to release pain from our own childhood, we discover many things about how we can relate to our children, even when the children have grown up.

By guiding adults back to memories from their childhood, I have learnt quite a lot about how the soul energy in us works. Seemingly trivial incidents seen with adult eyes may feel very painful and form big consequences for the life of a child. The following example shows a situation that probably lasted for only a short while. For the 3 year old it coloured his personality and self-perception as an adult. When the patterns come forth by realising their feelings, the clients discover how they have limited themselves by subconscious feelings. That is when inner doors open.

An example about how a short lasting pain may imprint life

A client with neck problems came to me to learn to use the keys. I call him John. He lied down to relax in his entire body. When he was totally relaxed, he moved his attention to his chest where his soul is cen-

tered. He instantly got up the memory where the pain had its root. His inner child took him to the time when he as 3 years old boy had got a sister. John had got a lot of attention when his mother came home with the baby. He was allowed to hold her and be the proud big brother. To start with his parents had been aware that he needed to be seen. But then, an uncle and aunt came to visit. They brought gifts for the mother and the baby and they gave all their attention to the new child when visiting.

The three year old felt ignored, but was at the same time too proud to beg for attention so he crawled behind an armchair where he sat quiet as a mouse while he listened to what the adults were talking about. They were concentrated on the small one and things that we talk about when a child is born; how big she was, who she resembled, which colour her eyes were etc. The aunt was allowed to hold the baby. He could not hear that they asked for him at all. They had completely forgotten him. He sat there and got heartbroken deep inside. He felt that nobody cared about him any more. He felt that what he was so proud about, to hold his little sister, was taken from him. He felt that the small one took his place. He felt that nobody cared about what he felt. His nature was to sit still and say nothing. He locked a big amount of feelings inside during the time that passed until his mother was aware that her three year old wasn't present. They called for him and he came forth from his hiding place without being able to say anything. He wasn't able to express his feelings, but locked them inside and pretended that he was OK. He had only looked at them with a serious glance and concluded that they had got a new child who got all the attention. Then he was taken up on someone's lap and got attention and his parents must have thought that he was all right.

When this man was my client, I discovered something very important about feelings. The feelings he had the short while he had been sitting behind the armchair, became a repeating pattern inside, even if he was taken care of and comforted shortly after. What the three year old had concluded was the way he experienced life for a little while only. That was going to characterize parts of his life until that day he released it.

For how long he was sitting there is not possible to say, but John and I agreed that it was likely a short time — maybe only five minutes. At the start of the guidance when I met John, I got some information about his life in the introductory conversation. After a few minutes I got a picture of how he felt that there was no room for him and how he felt that he was unappreciated in the eyes of others even if he had good results in his work. It emerged the way he expressed himself. Such patterns are often shown in clauses after a 'but', a 'because' or a 'maybe' where we excuse or explain how we are doing in life. In this case I know that my client found several parallels where he had created similar situations and reinforced the pattern through his life.

This example shows that children's perception about life starts to be formed at an early age, before the child has the ability to draw logical conclusions at the mind level. The way we are brought up usually colours families from generation to generation. We all want to be good parents. The good ways we remember from our parents' upbringing often become our own ways. In the very most cases I think we as parents avoid the ways that made life difficult. We learn no doubt from generation to generation.

Still, all parents have been children and carry along their own feelings and patterns of reactions that form their ways of being – as parents too. That is one of the reasons I warmly recommend even young people to work with the keys. It is a great learning experience… as a school in education. By understanding yourself and your own background, you get unique insights about life. However, it isn't necessarily what you enjoyed in your childhood that is the best way of bringing up your own children! This is where the challenge is. Parents are responsible for providing their children versatile and instructive experiences – where they are naturally present. Good parents experience things together with their children, but they also are confident that their children can learn and develop being with other adults. Upbringing is not only coloured by family culture, but by trends and attitudes in society and whether the parents have a religious belief or not.

Society has changed so much during the last 30 years that upbringing seems to be a big challenge for today's parent generation. I am old enough not to have experienced my children sitting in front of addictive computer games. Therefore, I don't have personal experiences of how this feels. TV and computer games, to a certain degree are passivating, but what does it lead to for the soul to be in another world during parts of the day and night? What value systems do the different games and programs represent? For the child soul's naive nature the world experienced on the screen may become a part of reality – or the entire reality so that the child doesn't relate to life itself. I have actually experienced pupils in school that related to figures from TV as if they are a part of their lives. It may happen when both the soul and the mind exchange reality and fiction. I think TV and computer games influence children much more than what researchers have found until now. For me it was like an adventure when I was allowed to go to the cinema at 7 years old. – A Danish 'Father to four' movie that made a great impression. The scary was very scary and was stuck in me for a long time. The joyful gave me many impulses to play.

An example of the parental relationship

A lady came to me for guidance. During the introductory conversation she told me about how her father was important for her and how good he was at things. Yet I felt that there was something that was not right. When I suggested that she ought to take a look at the relationship to her father, she claimed hotly that she didn't need that at all. Yet she was open to relax and let her soul show her the way towards what she needed to look at. Her soul took her directly to a situation where as a 13 year old girl she had been furious with her father for not letting her go out with high heels and a mini skirt. She had to realize that whilst being back in the memory, she was full of feelings that she didn't have any idea that she had. She felt that her father didn't respect her. She had to do what her father told her, or he would stop giving her weekly pocket money. She said out loud all feelings coming up and realized that she had made an agreement with herself about doing what her father demanded – to use low shoes and skirts to her knees until she was 16 years old. Her family was prosperous and she always got plenty of pocket money, so money was more important than the personal choice about skirt and shoes.

When she looked back at this, she discovered that the contract she made had created a pattern related to money. She discovered that she had realised a sentence about a feeling, which was exactly what was repeated in her life. 'I realise that I feel that I would rather have money than to do as I want for myself'. She had to admit that she often let money decide the choices that she made in many areas of her life. She could also see that she had an issue relating to the men throughout her life. She had to ad-

mit that she was able to remember the memory, but hadn't given it any significance because she loved her father. After having worked through the memory, she realised that the feelings in the memory had influenced her life for many years. The anger she had felt when her father decided over her, she had put a lid on and chosen to compensate for by money.

My conclusion is that we cannot let love for our parents prevent us from release work. Maybe love for our family is the reason we really should do it. A man told me he was certain he had nothing to release related to his parents because he regarded them as perfect parents. I wonder? If you have such an attitude to other people, either parents or others, you need to stop and think. Nobody is perfect. What does it mean to be perfect? We don't need to be perfect parents either. We need to be our best. We are humans and it's human to fail – and it is human to forgive and love each other even if we sometimes do stupid things we regret.

An example that shows how even small incidents may form our psyche

I was searching for the reason I didn't dare to get properly paid for pictures that I had made. It showed up to be a childhood memory that led me to understand why. When I was 6 years old and was sent to a hardware store to buy a spatula, the shop was sold-out of spatulas. It was late autumn because on the counter were some colourful gingerbread biscuit moulds. I had never seen anything like them before. This was in the 50s, at a time when plastic products started to show up in the shops. The creativity and joy in me took over and with radiating eyes I bought a blue and red one instead of the spatula! I am certain I had a guilty conscience on my way home because I was a well-behaved child, but the joy with the colourful shapes and what we could do with them was stronger. I am sure my mother got a bit resentful when I came home without a spatula, but then she laughed and thought it was funny. This is a story she has told several times through my life because she thought it was enjoyable *and she has remembered it when it was time for cookie baking. When I related to that memory, it turned out to be a Gordian knot* that had deep roots and that was triggered by the situation. Therefore it was important to dissolve. I felt I was ridiculed for something I was proud and happy about, but at the same time I knew I had done something wrong. It made me make a link between joy and guilt. I had to work very thoroughly with everything I felt. I made sentences that included both my spontaneity and the feeling of being ridiculed and to have done it because of my creative joy.*

13 Important features of the human nature

It is usual to push away negative thoughts and feelings, so when I explain to people I meet how their feelings create physical pain, they usually don't want to listen. Still, they may start talking about having pain in their back a minute later. It seems that they think that pain occurs by itself as if it is an inevitable part of human nature. I do understand that it feels painful and difficult to face bad feelings, but when I know how our feelings cause physical pain, I cannot let go of explaining the coherence.

Most people I meet have a kind of mechanical perception about their body and they want to avoid pain. They often say fatigue or calcification is the reason for their pain or they say it is psychosomatic. I am convinced that even what is perceived as pain because of fatigue, may be cured if one works with the feelings that prevent the life energy in the unpleasant area. The cells have to a large extent, the ability to repair themselves when life energy is fully present. To make that happen you must also remove the thought that fatigue is the reason and be confident that you recover totally. Remember, the life energy is love so we need to remove thoughts and feelings that prevent us from appreciation and love for ourselves.

When physical pain is strong, painkilling tablets are necessary. We cannot release the reasons behind strong pain over night. If you have pain in your body, you need to assume that it takes time to find the root causes. Whichever pain it is, it doesn't occur in your body by coincidence. Pain and illness always have a reason and the reasons may be deep and troublesome and you may have the need to reduce the pain for a while. There is nothing wrong in taking painkillers and working with the Keys of liberation at the same time. However, our cells don't have free will, so they continue to repeat the pain until what is aching is released. Remember to tell your soul not to enhance when having pain! Explain that enhancing leads to the pain enhancing too.

You might suddenly get better. Your soul may release without your mind being present, so that your condition suddenly improves. Your soul may learn from other souls and realise things at a subconscious level. This might happen when you are honest with yourself about what you feel during your daily life.

In most cases, it is emotional wounds coming up when we use the keys. They have made us compensate by choosing many different solutions to avoid the pain repeating itself. In some cases we may have done bad things on purpose. Or we might not have understood that what we did caused pain in others. It doesn't need to be serious things, but it creates avoidance mechanisms and self-denial. This might be things we have done and we need to admit that we were dishonest, cowardly, arrogant or stupid. When we choose to face it and to acknowledge what we did wrong, it is as if we lift huge burdens from our shoulders.

Situations in your past that were painful when they happened may not be as bad as you think. It actually feels good to cry to empty yourself and it is liberating. If you try to realise what you feel one day when something happens that knocks you out, the insight you get will be big enough to work as a driving force to continue to take your unpleasant feelings seriously. You might discover that it's an idea to make 'key work' a part of your life?

When in our daily life we get angry, annoyed, insulted, criticise others or similar, it is often our own wounds that are triggered that make us react. A person may remind you about another person who once hurt you. For you who often are annoyed by other people, I recommend you get started in using the keys to find out what it is about others that annoys you. It may be your own ways of behavior in earlier situations that are hidden from you, that make you annoyed. In other words, you may be annoyed at yourself.

I have discovered that it is almost always our own well hidden baggage of inferiority that is the reason we criticize and think negatively about others. It is often our own feeling of guilt that makes us place blame outside of ourselves. What is painful to feel, we have the tendency to notice in others. This is called projecting*. Our human psyche is put together in a way so that it's not easy to see our own emotional baggage because of our tendency to push away what feels bad. It is so much easier to see mistakes with others than with ourselves. When partners break up, it's often because such mechanisms have started to work. If you realize that this and you start using the realizing key on what feels difficult in the relationship, you may get aha-experiences that bring you in harmony with your partner again. The key word is to dare to be honest with yourself.

An example about projecting

A lady who is an eager 'key-user' called me to get help with finding clarity in her relation to a colleague. Over time her relationship to the lady who had the office next to her had worsened. She was upset because she had not been able to find out what this was about. This was what came up when she started to use the first key:

I realise that I feel stepped on.
I realise that I get furious because she says the words I would have said.
I realise that I feel that she is ruining things for me.
I realise that I feel that I am never able to keep things for myself.
I realise that I feel that she always wants things her way.

That helped. She had to admit that this was something she needed to look at in her own subconscious. The colleague had not violated her intentionally or knowingly done anything that would indicate that she had reason to be annoyed or feel overrun. She realised that she reacted because the colleague reminded her of how her mother had raised her. It suddenly came up in passing while we talked. Then she immediately understood what she wanted to grab hold of to release.

She worked her way through the current situation in relation to the colleague with all four keys and felt that the relationship with the colleague was understood and much easier to handle. Later she took hold of the relationship with her mother in certain situations she remembered from her childhood when she had felt similar things as related to the colleague, in the present. After the unpleasant feelings were released, she became best friends with her colleague.

When we think negatively about others who succeed or are happy, it's our own wounds that make us do so. This is what we call envy. If you once have experienced not succeeding with something you have worked hard to achieve but that everything worked against you, it may hurt so much that you always get negative thoughts about those who succeed.

An example about how the feeling of not being good enough led to negative thoughts about others

I had had tension in my hips since I was a young girl. One particular day I got the impulse to go to a meeting to listen to a lady giving a speech. As I was sitting, listening to the person speaking, I had thoughts that I always wanted to get rid of. These were negative thoughts about the person who was speaking. I tried to think positively, I admired her dress and I saw that she was a beautiful person. Simultaneously I could not let go of being critical again. I knew this was an awakening call for me. My negative pattern was shown to me! When I thought back, my hips and thighs very often were very tense when seeing performances of all kinds. As I was sitting listening that day I suddenly knew that I was thinking negatively about skillful people.

When I got home, I immediately lay down and went into that part of my body, knowing that there had to be a secret waiting for me. The picture coming up was from the gymnastic group I joined when I was 14 years of age. One day a new leader was presented to the group. She was a skillful person who wanted to make a competing group of the best girls. She observed us all, and at the end of the training she picked out the best girls she wanted to give extra training to. At that time we were three friends, nearly always hanging together... my two best friends were picked out to be in this elite group. I wanted so much to be in the group with them, so I asked this new leader if I could join and she said it was all right. During the next months I exercised really hard, I tried the best I could to be as good as the others... gymnast exercises, however, weren't really the thing for me, and one day the leader came to me after the training and asked me not to come to the gymnast training any more. This was the moment of total disaster. The pain and shame I felt was so total, so awful that I simply could not feel it... I immediately locked the feelings into my system, into my body where I created a thought pattern that I carried for almost 40 years! When the picture came up, I went back to the place, the atmosphere of the locker room of the gymnasium and the eyes of the other girls. I went into the feelings and repeated and repeated everything until I felt it all dissolve and I was set free, and the energy started to flow... Many tears were shed, but a wonderful feeling spread throughout my body accompanying the releasing work. By this experience I discovered how envy occurs. Deep wounds of not feeling good enough had created it. Eventually I travelled many journeys into my hips until the pain left me.

As soon as we encounter situations that remind us about it, negative thoughts about the people who trigger the memory come up. It can be anything, not only personal relations and situations that trigger such feelings. It happens just as much when we watch TV or movies, read the newspaper or attend performances of different kinds. When you think negatively about people you don't know or who do positive things, these are warning lamps. Then it's a very good reason to use the realising key on what you feel. Be honest with yourself and you find out that it's not about them, but about you. In most cases, you get up memories where you didn't succeed, where you felt betrayed or where you felt that the others were much better than you etc.

Another archetypical* feature of our psyche is to feel that others are better than us – or we feel better than others. This has led us to estimate things as better than and less than so we compare everything. It has created a competing mentality that makes it necessary to ask ourselves; is this the way we want our society to be? Do we want to compete on everything? Does it really bring out the best in us? Or does it create losers? Do the competing systems create better societies? Do we achieve better lives? Maybe it is better to compete with ourselves? I think our tendency to compare will decrease as people get an insight through releasing their personal luggage. Deep inside, most of us think in ways that make us look up to someone. Someone may have the tendency to lean on someone who is better and cleverer than themselves, while others have the need to look up to someone they can idolize. On the other hand, many of us tend to look down at groups or individuals who in one way or another are standing out. These ways are what I call archetypical*. I have discovered that they have roots from the original soul energies, far back in time, but that all people carry them from generation to generation because many of our souls are of ancient origin. I am convinced that this will decrease because of growing awareness about self-development in the decades to come. In the long term it will lead to more and more people having the ability to think and act equally and fairly, without the need for comparing and estimating.

A feature that seems to be usual for many people is that we feel that we need to be perfect. Must we? For a long time I was like that. Actually I had not thought about it until one day as an assistant professor I had a demanding workshop day with experienced teachers. After finishing the day there was evaluation and I was given flowers. They were content. The evaluation questionnaire showed that all but two said 'very good' about my teachings. One was 'good' and the last person was neutral. Still, sitting on the plane on my way home, an unpleasant feeling came up in me. When I went deeply into my feelings, I discovered to my surprise that the reason for my sadness was the two participants who weren't super-content. My rational mind was very content with the day, but my soul felt heavy. It was an irrational feeling. When I got home, I looked deeply into my feelings and found that I had a basic pattern about having to be perfect. I thought I had to be perfect for someone to love me. Many small episodes from my childhood emerged. They gave me aha-experiences about how the old way of upbringing by 'the carrot principle' had worked in me. 'Now you need to be good, and you will have…' 'Now you have to eat it all, and then you will get dessert'. – And little me was obedient and did what I was told in most cases. It gave me a basic feeling about having to be good to make my parents happy about me. Several years later I found an underlying cause of this pattern in myself, which turned out to be one of my main patterns. It was created by memories where I felt I was not good enough the way I am. That feeling made me always feel that I needed to please other people. This is also what I call an archetypical pattern, being common in many people.

I have discovered that the reason for many people's patterns is this: To feel that we need to be perfect to succeed… to be loved… to be liked. Most of us don't reflect on it, but this is one of the subconscious convictions caused by religions, that have been inherited from generation to generation. This is one of the reasons the word acceptance has such a strong effect. When we accept ourselves the way we are, instead of comparing with ideals, new doors open.

In the philosophical study we found that life energy allows life to unfold, without judging. It doesn't contain guilt or feelings of not being good enough. It is we who have the tendency to feel guilt, to judge and criticize ourselves and each other because of the wounds in our souls. When we realize that everybody does their best under the circumstances, related to their beliefs and the greater school of life, we discover that it becomes constantly easier to accept that we are different. We don't always know what other people feel and think, but we know that we are in this together; we are all in the same boat. Can you imagine that as people begin to think in this way, we begin to reason differently about life? Do you think more and more people eventually may take responsibility for their lives in new ways so that they give each other freedom from accusations?

14 The relationship to ourselves and to each other

I thought I had to be perfect to accept myself. It was very difficult to accept my belly and my chocolate eating… However, it was exactly what I had to do to get on. Many among us need to a larger extent to face ourselves. It's because we have patterns that make us criticize and judge ourselves. We try to hide what we don't want to see. Acceptance benefits us because the life energy is accepting. It is important to see this perspective because acceptance of ourselves makes the life energy become stronger. Our body gets happy by getting acknowledgement.

Another characteristic of the life energy is to allow life to unfold so that every single choice we contribute to gives life direction. If the choices we do make us gain weight or become smokers, it's better to accept it than to bother oneself with negative thoughts about it, because that limits the life energy. When we understand that it is our emotional wounds that make us do things that don't serve, we can get started with the Keys of liberation and the reasons for the problem get smaller as we discover and release the emotions that created it. Then it becomes easy to stop smoking and to loose weight! When we expect something to happen, our thoughts are contributing to what will happen. If we expect something positive, positive things are supposed to happen, but if our subconscious patterns caused by fear and inferiority say the opposite, it does not happen. If we are pessimists because of our emotional wounds, it influences our lives in a negative direction. Therefore, knowledge about how the subconscious patterns work is important for everybody.

The thing is, we don't really notice whether the thoughts are our own or whether we pick up other people's perception through the energy field. They are experienced as our own. When someone who means much to us wants us to agree with them, their thoughts may influence us more than we are aware of. The same applies to strong personalities who think they are right. Before you know it, you have joined something that you did not really agree to. If we don't know what is happening energetically, we cannot do anything about it. What serves is to be true to ourselves and to clean up in our own lives. We need to stand up for what we think is right. It is time people understand that thoughts not only are located in the head, but everywhere around us. Of course it is still important to listen to what others have to say.

By being aware of our thoughts and by observing ourselves and our surroundings in our daily lives we get far. Don't let heavy thoughts about yourself pull you down because now you are about to learn about how you can start acting upon your emotions with good tools. New possibilities will open, not only for you personally, but you will discover that you start observing all of existence from a new angle. Not least of all, you will discover how important it is to think and express positively. Notice how nice words create a good climate in all situations both for others and for you.

There are many types of feelings that don't serve, that create energetic bonds between us and other people. In reality this means that we keep other people stuck in our opinion about how we think they should be. Things aren't necessarily the way we think and feel about them. Except when we bring up children, we normally have no responsibility for other people's choices.

Many people may experience such bonds as positive because it feels secure and it's the way we are used to. However, when we are too strongly attached to another human being, none of us are happy. It is usually about relations between parents and children (both ways), between siblings and between spouses/partners. It can also occur between good friends.

Concrete situations that make us feel something related to other people may mean that we carry their feelings and subconscious thoughts. On several occasions I have guided people having physical pain that turned out to belong to someone else. You may discover if this is the case with you when you start realising what you feel. If what you feel doesn't fit with your mind's perception of what happened, but is an expression of the person that caused your pain, you carry their feelings. What happens is that we subconsciously carry something that belongs to others. It may be the way others have treated us or brought us up. We may also put our energy on others so that they carry a burden on our behalf. This may happen very subtly and without our conscious notice of it. What we do then is not logical but the soul's way of reacting.

Guilt, guilty conscience, bitterness, need to blame, worry, responsibility, expectations, longing and obligation are feelings that bind humans together in unfortunate ways. It may also happen when someone loves another person too much and forgets themselves. All these feelings create bonds when we feel them related to other people. In most cases, it doesn't serve to let other people's feelings decide our lives. It doesn't serve anyone to take decisions for others who are adults and able to take responsibility for themselves, their feelings, thoughts and actions.

Of course, the best way is to find out about such conditions in your life and to talk with the people you are related to. It isn't always easy to know how, because this may be a problem at a subconscious level. Think thoroughly through your life. Is there anyone you make decisions for? Is there anyone you feel responsible for that ought to take responsibility for themselves? Do you think it might happen that the person isn't able to take responsibility because you take it from them, completely or partially? Maybe someone takes responsibility for you so that you don't do things that are your responsibility in some areas of your life? Maybe you become lazy because of that? Could it be that you take things too easy because there is someone who comes and cleans up after you?

If you experience a person often wants to give you things for no reason, it might be a sign of guilty conscience. Think through the relation to the person. Maybe you discover more situations indicating the same. It is most likely that the reason is in the subconscious. It may be due to the person's emotional baggage and behavior, and it may have roots far back in time.

If you don't manage to speak to another person face to face, you can speak to their soul. The person you want to set yourself free from or you want to set free from you, doesn't need to know about it if you feel it is too difficult. You can speak to their soul this way: You close your eyes and visualise that the person sits in front of you, and then you speak to the person as if he/she is present. In reality you speak to their soul that represents their feelings, values and qualities. Our souls are connected at the soul level and when you do this with sincerity, their soul will perceive what you say. It is important that you are honest both with yourself and with the person you relate to and that you really want to end the imbalanced state between you.

An example about carrying another person's energy

We perceive things differently at the soul level and in our conscious mind. A friend who uses the Keys told me that he had worked through a memory that happened when he was about 6 years old. He had been playing football with some boys but it was late and they had gone home so he was alone at the house. He saw his father coming and thought happily: 'Dad is coming to play football with me. Now I will show him how good I am'. But his father didn't want to play football. He only wanted to get his son to bed. So he pulled him along with him to get him home… The boy became quiet and sullen and at the soul level he had done the follow-

ing: He took from his father his responsibility of upbringing. His soul, which is an old soul, regarded himself as wise and thought his father was stupid as he didn't understand how important it was to make time for his son. Until this release work that he did at 35 years of age, he had taken from his father his responsibility as a father. Now he gave it back.

Think thoroughly through what makes you behave and think the way you do. Tell the person clearly what you think and feel. For ex. if your mother always wants to say her opinion when you are deciding something, she doesn't let you have your free will. You can make up your opinion about why it is that way, and you can speak to her soul the way it is described here and explain that you are adult and fully have the ability to make your own choices. Be caring and decisive.

Through release work I have learned how important it is to be neutral in certain situations. When you have worked through feelings for a while, you will see such situations and take a step back and consider instead, taking part in conflicts. Eventually you develop a greater ability to neutralize and learn by observing and reflection instead of increasing conflicts by taking part in them.

15 Irrational patterns

The soul has not got the same logical ability to reason the way the mind has. This is the reason it is usual to react irrationally in many situations. For example if something turned out totally wrong in a situation once you really felt you succeeded in something you like doing, you get afraid that things might turn out wrong so when you try to do something you really like to do, you get paralysed by *anxiety**. An irrational pattern could be: When you want to do things your own way because you know you can, you get depressed. The irrational patterns occur in situations when the soul has drawn conclusions based on previous wounds so that an illogical conviction is formed in the psyche. It functions as a rule, as lawfulness. These situations are often such that the soul isn't willing to listen to the logic of the mind until we thoroughly shed light upon the irrational aspect of it. We can do that by moving back in time, realising exactly the contradictory feelings we felt at the time when the pattern occurred. Just after something dreadful happens the first time, we are not able to work through the feelings. We need to cry, to react, to mourn. Eventually we need to see, realise and understand our feelings. (see example of anxiety, page...)

What I call a *Gordian knot** is a pattern that occurs when we have a positive intention and experience a negative outcome. Such situations can become subconscious "rules" like this: "When I do my very best, something happens that makes me fail". Or "When I am content with myself, there's always someone who turns against me". Or "When I am proud of being clever, people say I am stupid".

What happens psychologically is that the soul repeats these 'lawfulnesses' as if it is the way it is. As if it is true! Then it becomes that way at the subconscious level in the person's life. The soul has its own thoughts that subconsciously repeat the pain. This leads to a situation where the soul repeats itself and creates new irrational situations that resemble the first and that reinforce the same kind of feelings.

An example of how a Gordian knot is formed

Little Lucy, 5 years old, is eager and happy sitting in the sandpit with her friend of the same age. The two have made roads and houses and used leaves, grass and flowers to create a garden and wooden sticks for walls. They are engaged and play continuously for hours without noticing time. Then a big boy comes along. He has been scolded and is very upset so is he mad at the whole world. When he sees the two happy children in the sandbox, he simply drives through their creation with his bike. Lucy's world collapses, literally. Not only is their creation destroyed, but Lisa's soul is devastated. When mom comes to take her home, Lucy is dissolved in tears and rages with despair. Her mother does as well as she can and says that they will create new roads and houses in the sandpit the next day. Lucy eventually calms down. Then she becomes very quiet and withdraws into herself, because her soul has concluded: 'When I am eager and happy, creating together with the one I love, a disaster happens'. She cannot put it into words – she might lock it inside of herself as a deep grief about life itself.

As you can see, this is "an everyday situation" in an adult's eyes. Still, it may form Lisa's life, both when growing up and when she becomes adult. Because: Lucy's subconscious will repeat the pain and several similar feelings she had when the disaster happened. When Lucy later in life is happy and eagerly creating together with the man she loves, things might happen that destroys the happiness. It may happen during adolescence, it may happen several times in her adult life. And Lucy doesn't understand why the things in her life go wrong every time she really feels fine together with a partner.

We all have similar knots in our psyche to a smaller or larger extent. When we go back to painful situations we must find out if they may contain Gordian knots. Then we have to include both the positive, good intention/feeling and the negative result in one and the same realizing sentence. Then we are able to "unlock" the lawfulness so that our soul understands that this is not our truth. One such sentence is usually not enough because in most cases there are several feelings related to the 'catastrophe'. When we work with such knots, we need to recognise all the feelings thoroughly and exactly the way we feel so that the sentences that express the irrational pain are totally precise. Then we use the inner child technique when we move back to the memory and hold our arms around ourselves, applying forgiveness and love. To forgive those who caused such painful experiences is important, even if we don't know the person, like in this example.

There are other types of knots in our inner beings I call *Contradiction knots**. They occur when a soul meets another value system than their own so that a conflict occurs between what the person believes is right and what important persons in their life belief and stand for. This often happens in our lives at the age of

2-4 years when we adapt to our parents demands and their perception of our upbringing. As small children we have the love, joy and trust as a guideline in life. Many of the things that our parents see as matters of course are almost impossible to understand for the child. When we are small and they are our parents, they should represent love, safety and anchoring. Then, when they need to put limits for us, they start representing value systems that feel contradictory to our perception. Thus contradiction knots occur in our psyche.

An example: When you feel that those representing love in your life are strict and say: 'Eat up your food, now!' Maybe they don't allow you to play, but get you to the table even if you are not in the least hungry. As a child soul you may ask: 'Why do I need to do that?' It ends (often after anger, grief and despair) with that you give in and let your parents decide because they are big and represent safety and love.

In such situations our soul may get wounds by feeling: "I am not good enough the way I am" or 'I feel grief because I am not allowed to decide for myself'. What recognises a contradiction knot is that we have feelings related to our own value system and related to a value system that someone else has put upon us: "I feel that it is my fault that my mother is angry because I don't want to eat".

Contradiction knots also occur in situations where we as adults feel that we are pushed or fooled into other value systems, for instance when it comes to religion or policy. Maybe you attended something to be a part of the gang? Perhaps it meant doing or meaning something you didn't agree with. Still you went on because otherwise you felt you would loose the friends and the community you were a part of? My advice is: Be true to yourself and what you know within is right and true to you. Be honest to you feelings! If it is too tough to say out loud what you mean, you can withdraw from the situation and apply the Keys to the feelings that make you not dare to say what you mean. Then you will probably dare it at a later occasion. If you stand up for your opinions and give the reason for them, you will always be listened to... unless you have patterns saying: "No one wants to listen to me..." or "Nobody thinks what I say is important..." It is very important to understand how subconscious patterns form limiting mechanisms between humans. It makes humans hold each other in certain perceptions.

Contradiction knots may also have their roots in earlier lives. I have seen this, especially with people who during counselling have experienced moving back to being religious people in middle age. The souls wanted to live in love, freedom, creativity and joy, but they believed in a god that demanded from them to be true to strict and irrational demands.

An example of a contradiction knot

'I have released a childhood memory of a life in the middle ages when I was put in a convent school. I was about 5–6 years old. Earlier in that life I had experienced seeing a juggler troupe where people in colorful clothes were dancing, singing and playing theatre. It was the greatest spectacle I had ever experienced! I had an enormous joy and longing in me to do the same as them. The first thing that happened when I came to the convent school, was to be taken to the church. I discovered immediately the wonderful echo in the room. Full of joy, I spontaneously started to sing, which was not suitable according to the rules of the church. The consequence was that I was punished in the most awful way, close to torture, because I didn't show god decent behavior. It led eventually to me being a less nice person to relate to in that life. My experience is that contradiction knots should be released in this way: First release the feelings related to your own soul's belief system and then the feelings related to what you thought you had to do. In this case I first released the grief because singing was forbidden and felt despair because I wasn't allowed to express my

joy spontaneously. *Then I released the despair over feeling sinful for not adhering to God's commandments. It is absolutely necessary to sort out parts of ourselves to get through emotions and achieve the insight that follows. Contradiction knots really feel like tangles in one's inner self. It was a great relief the day I released that memory and subsequent experiences'.*

Another phenomenon that I have discovered in our psyche, I call *coupling**. It occurs when we relate a situation, a way of being, a habit, a smell, a melody with certain feelings. Couplings can also relate some feelings to other types of feelings, for ex. I discovered that I had a pattern where I related love to guilt.

I mean that couplings may lead to obsessions or compulsive behavior. It happens when we associate a feeling with certain things or phenomenon so that we have to do it to feel good. It is an irrational feeling that comes to the surface as conscious thoughts or compulsively manifests as a physical action. When we use the Keys systematically and thoroughly and include exactly what we feel/think in the sentences, we are in most cases able to set ourselves free from such couplings. You have to assume that it takes more than one key work to get to the bottom of it. However, it is beneficial to know the phenomenon so that you can unlock the irrational lawfulness by including all parts of the thoughts / emotions when realising.

An example of a coupling

This is about a client who had asthma. Let us call her Martha. I have experienced that problems with the lungs may represent self pity. In this case it was a guide line for what I could help her to find out. She wanted to stop smoking. Simultaneously she remarked, that being able to blame the asthma when she could not manage to go as far as others, worked well for her. Maybe it works best for me to be a convenience zone, she said honestly about herself. That put us on track. When Martha went back to the memory she found herself in the cradle as a baby! Both parents smoked and at that time there was no thought of how the baby felt. The baby was lying in the cradle and pitied herself, so she related tobacco smoke with the feeling of self pity.

This is in itself a coupling. Therefore we discovered that one of the reasons she didn't manage to stop smoking was that she felt good about the fact that people pitied her so that she could be in the 'convenience zone'. The little child was lying in the cradle, bothered by the parents' smoking and experienced grief and despair because her parents didn't heed her. Even if this was before she could speak, she repeated in her thoughts, "I feel sorry for myself because I'm an involuntary smoker". That was the sentence coming up when she started to realize what she felt in the memory. However, even if Martha applied the Keys to this, she didn't manage to stop smoking. There turned out to be several things she related emotionally to the smoking of her parents.

The parents tried to put the baby in another room where there was no smoke, but then Martha felt lonely and forgotten by her parents. As a baby she got a dilemma between being inside the smoky living room where she felt loved – or being in the cool, quiet bedroom, but there she felt lonely. Then it dawned on Martha as an adult, she began to realize the situations in which she needed a cigarette. That was when she needed comfort! However, simultaneously the smoke gave her a feeling of pitying herself. This way she made a double coupling, a roundel that was difficult to get out of. Martha used to call me to get help when she had a hard time. One day she had to admit that she always had to smoke when calling me... that was the leading thread, opening new doors.

It showed up to be yet one more coupling to the smoking. When she was lying in the cradle, she decided never to smoke. Being an old soul, she actually made a positive contract with herself as a baby. When in her teens, together with a friend who wanted to try to smoke, she had bought cigarettes and went up in the wood to smoke but pretended that she was her father... and avoided the contract she had done with herself. So the challenge for her as an adult was to set herself free from her father's ways of thinking.

Some of the most difficult things a human being can experience are sexual abuse. Then there are almost always both Gordian knots and contradiction knots to release. It is because the abuser often is someone the person loves and because sexual feelings are pleasant so that there may be an offence related to positive feelings/desire. I have guided many women that have been abused sexually. Common for most of them is the feeling of being offended and abused and simultaneously feel that it could be physically pleasant against their will. Such contradictory feelings are very difficult for those who have experienced this. In addition, society has condemned all kinds of sexual attraction between adults and children so those who tell about abuse are "committed" to feel infringement only. In addition, the one who experience abuse also may have a sense of solidarity and love for the person she violates.

When someone works with releasing sexual abuse, it is very important to recognise that there might have been good feelings also. Those women I have helped to realise such feelings, felt a great relief to hear that many other women feel the same way. This is very important to release in realising sentences where one includes both the pain by being offended and the feeling of liking the sexual feeling. When this is the case, one needs to reflect on whether there are contradictions related to being offended by someone that one loves – and compassion/solidarity with the caring person. My experience is that such contradictions may dissolve when working thoroughly and precisely and realizing and forgiving all feelings and couplings between feelings that form irrational "lawfulness" in the psyche. When one works to release sexual abuse, it is important to be true to oneself first of all and work through all feelings where both positive and negative feelings are included in the same sentence. Then you can bring forth feelings related to solidarity with the abuser. It is important to take time and not necessarily to do it all at once, but let time work for you. If you have started to relate to such issues and the assault has taken place over a long time, you need to give yourself many possibilities to release as it brings up memories in you. Meanwhile you should know that your soul sees and understands things that it releases at the soul level so that it eases the pressure.

An example of how sexual abuse may lead to carrying another person's feelings

This is from a counselling of a young lady who had been sexually abused by a close relative. She had put a lid on it and started to remember it when she attended a workshop with me. She had repressed the abuse since she was a child, but when she started to realize what she felt, the memories came to the surface. When she started to work through the strong feelings, she discovered that it wasn't her own anger she was carrying. We discovered that she had taken the man's anger from him so that he would not be violent to her. By working through every feeling coming up in her and by speaking to the abuser's soul, she set herself free. She imagined that he sat in front of her and she told him everything she felt, and then she gave him back all the feelings she had taken away from him when the abuse happened, so that he would be able to feel his feelings and release them when he one day would be ready for it. I witnessed an enormously tough process. She was very determined to free herself from the pain, so she made it. She continued to release on her own and when I met her a year later she was like a new human being.

By using the Keys of liberation thoroughly related to sexual abuse, you can set yourself totally free from all long lasting pain. For example, a client who had been abused by her father for several years and who had brought him to court, wanted to contact him and to tell him that she had forgiven him.

16 Emotional pain from earlier lives

Some irrational feelings and response patterns are very difficult to find out about unless we are willing to realise that we have lived before. Earlier lives may have a major impact on the life we live now. If for example in a life you have been a priest or a monk and given the promise of celibacy, and failed to keep the promise because you fell in love, the memory would likely be triggered by something that happens in your youth. Feelings and ways of thinking of that life will be with you and influence you in this life. The feelings and ways of thinking from that life will then contribute to colour your ways in this life.

If you in an earlier life experienced dying in childbirth, it will color your relation to how you treat your children in this life. Probably you are irrational and are afraid to let them down, so you might make strong bonds to them.

Many souls choose to incarnate in the same family so that the children in an earlier life may be their children in this life. Our souls may also choose other family constellations. Our souls choose what they mean gives the best learning. It may result in good relations, but it may also lead to feelings and situations that we don't understand when painful memories are triggered.

A journey back across time and space is called regression. Many years ago, when I started to get curious about earlier lives, I sought out a lady who offered regressions. It implied a directed consciousness journey back to memories of my soul. Such memories are actually stored in our cells. Our soul knows what we need to look for and we can therefore safely let us be led when we have good tools with which we can release the painful feelings. Liberation Keys are such tools.

An example of a regression

To start with I was led into a deeply relaxed condition. Then she asked me to put all my expectations aside, as if I took off some clothes and left them behind. Then she asked me to visualise a bridge and at the other side I would find what I needed to take a look at. I could not see anything when I had come across the bridge. Then she asked me to look at my feet and feel how they were… and suddenly I really was somewhere across time and space – back at another time and as another human being. I stood barefoot on an earth floor inside a cowshed without windows. She asked me to further turn around and to find the door and to exit. I did so and discovered that I came out into light, but it was also to a bleak feeling. It was a feeling of having been suppressed, having been stepped upon, actually bullied. There was a white house at the yard and that was certainly not where I wanted to go. I felt it was where bad people lived, so the therapist asked me to go to where I belonged and then I stepped to the left down along a track that led to a little cottage. That is where I lived with my mother. I understood that I was a cotter girl.

I remember the therapist asked many questions to circle into the memory, to make it clearer. One of the things that made me certain that this was a real memory, was when she asked me about what I was longing for most of all. It burst out of me before I got time to reflect: "To go to America!" There must have been someone I knew that had gone there and I knew that it had to be a good place. I would never have said it in a waken state in this life.

Then she asked me to move forward in time to the moment of death. Suddenly I was at a sawmill that was built above a waterfall. The next moment I saw myself lie on the rocks below the saw. I was a boy-like girl aged about 16 with far too short trousers, ragged shirt and a red cap. I had slipped and fell down and I was killed in the fall.

Then the therapist brought me back and I was lying on her divan in the present time. I could continue to lie to think through what I had experienced. The feeling of not being good enough, that always had accompanied me, was very prominent. I had the feeling that the people at the farm always criticised what I did and always wanted me to do more, even more than I actually managed. I felt that I was deathly tired when I died. I didn't dare to oppose them, because they would have been bad to my mother. Some years later, when I had started applying the Keys of liberation, I brought forth what I had experienced in the regression and I worked through feelings that had given me chronic pain in my hips through many years. Along the way I found that inferiority get stuck in the hips. Later I worked through several lives where that feeling was prominent. There were parallels in several earlier lives that contained the same pattern.

Last summer, when I was on my way from one valley to another in southern Norway I suddenly recognized where I had lived in that life and fell into tears. I was passing about where I had been living as a cotter girl. I felt I had to go out of the car to go for a walk in the landscape. Memories of having herded the cows from the farm in the mountains flowed through me. Up there, I had freedom. There were the cows and I was free from abuse. They were my friends.

Anxiety is an irrational fear that in most cases has roots in memories from earlier lives. My experience is that people who have anxiety have experienced something that triggered feelings with roots in an earlier life. This starts anxiety reactions that seem irrational and difficult to deal with. When we understand where it comes from, what happened and move back into the memory, the anxiety may dissolve rather quickly. Usually the person gets several aha-experiences when they are able to see the situation in an earlier life that created the fear in this life.

It is almost always such that we choose to incarnate together with souls whom we have lived with before. We do this first of all because of love for each other and because it feels safe. It leads to the wounds of the soul from earlier lives being triggered because we are the persons we are. There may be painful things that come to the surface because we didn't manage to forgive each other and died without having settled issues. In some cases the souls have not had the possibility to meet in another dimension in the meantime. Such old pain may contribute to form our lives and personality. Both from my own life path and from others I have met, I know that curiosity about earlier lives leads to a much more relaxed relationship to death. When we are certain that we live on in another dimension, we find tranquility.

Sometimes we meet people who we feel that we have met before but simultaneously we know that we haven't met them. Then it's usually about someone we knew in an earlier life. Sometimes these may be close relations and even the person you marry and have children with. Our souls actually make agreements to meet again and try to find each other at the physical level.

An example of the release of anxiety

About 10–12 years ago, I started to get more and more pain in my stomach. At that time I worked as an assistant professor at a college. It was a type of pain that was coming and going, so to start with I didn't think much about it. Reflecting on it today, I remember that I started to smoke more as the pressure got tougher. From being a party smoker, I started to take a cigarette when I felt the need to calm down. Simultaneously as I understood that it was anxiety, I didn't understand it. I noticed that some thoughts created pain being so strong that it felt like knives being stabbed in my stomach. Gradually I discovered that the worst pain was related to teaching, especially when teaching adult students. It was so bad that I could hardly move to the teaching room. When I had started classes it passed, because I loved my job. I concluded that it was triggered by adults who demanded something from me. Eventually I quit my job and moved to the countryside. I thought the anxiety would cease to create pain. – But no. Now it showed up when I had decided to go to the grocery shop. Eventually, half a year later I discovered what created the pain.

I did it by travelling by my thought into the pain in the stomach and holding it there. This time I got up a picture. The picture showed a wavy landscape and I understood that the colour symolised an old memory. I got the word Flanders. I knew at once that I hadn't been there in this life. It was as if I was shown a piece of something that was too painful to see and feel. I felt it had to be much older than any photograph.. Then I simply knew it, I sensed it; I was stoned by a crowd, a kind of lynching. Even if I could not feel the physical pain from the stones, I felt that I was stoned to death. The realisation came immediately. I felt I was a spiritual person in that life, a woman who went against what was told by the church. I had told a message that was incompatible with the religion of the middle ages and the stoning was a result of this.

What made me able to let go of the anxiety immediately was that I could see the parallel between that life and what I was doing at the time I got the anxiety. I had constantly taken more interest in spiritual thinking and was engaged in finding answers to the riddles of life across religions during the entire period I had growing anxiety. At the same time, I worked as a professor at the college where I felt that my thoughts about spiritual matters were not a topic of conversation. Now I understood why I in this life had been afraid of people that I knew a little, but who I didn't feel confident about. In the little town where this happened, we knew who everybody was. The people that stoned me were people that I knew. The anxiety disappeared the same day and never came back after I had seen and understood how it occurred. Later I was back there with the help of my pendulum* and released many feelings from that life that ended so tragically.

It is almost always so, that we choose to incarnate together with souls we have lived with before. We do that first of all because of love for each other and because it feels safe. It leads to that the wounds of the soul from earlier lives are being triggered because we are the persons we are. There may be painful things that come to the surface because we didn't manage to forgive each other and died without having settled. In some cases the souls have not had the possibility to meet in another dimension in the meantime. Such old pain may contribute to form our lives and personality. Both from my own life path and from others I have met, I know that curiosity about earlier lives leads to a much more relaxed relationship to death. When we are certain that we live on in another dimension, we find tranquility.

Sometimes we meet people who we feel that we have met before, but simultaneously we know that we haven't met. Then it's usually about someone we knew in an earlier life. Sometimes these may be close relations and even the person you marry and have children with. Our souls actually make agreements to meet again and try to find each other at the physical level.

17 Contracts we do with ourselves

When life goes against us and everything seems hopeless, it can be difficult to find courage to continue. I am certain that through your life you have been so angry and said that you have made what I call "contracts with yourself". Such contracts or decisions are more common than most people are aware of. We make them, for example when we say to ourselves: 'I shall never again…' 'I am never going there again'. 'It is unforgivable'. 'He can just wait…' 'I am always so unlucky…'

Reflect on this and you realise this is the way it is and you become more cautious about what you say. Such expressions that we all might have said are actually the guideline to our inner being. More examples: 'No, I'm so stupid, I can´t believe I can do such things'. 'No, that´s beyond me'. Do you recognise this? If you discover yourself saying such expressions, you are on your way to find something hidden in your subconscious. If you don't immediately remember where the negative expression about yourself comes from, I recommend using a pendulum* and ask if such a negative expression has roots in a memory. Such daily expressions show us the direction to find what we hide inside.

We may do such contracts both consciously and subconsciously. If that is the reason it is useful to notice what we say to other people in our daily talk. For example, if you have experienced being betrayed by a partner, in despair you might have said both to yourself and others: 'I shall never deal with women (men) ever again'. Such a sentence may easily become a truth and function as programming the particles you consist of, because even if you don't express it, your soul might have repeated it in anger and pain several times and thus it has become a truth. Then there will hardly be any of the opposite gender coming your way any more because it's the way you have decided life to be at a subconscious level of yourself.

Contracts with ourselves may also occur when we assure to others and to ourselves how we are upset about something that happened in our life. When we repeat and mean what we say several times, it is perceived by our cells as a programming! The cells we consist of we send out of us as our truth, and the same message is perceived subconsciously by people around us. Those people will then be co-creators to fulfil the programming. In this way new and similar situations where we get upset and angry occur. When we learn about how our psyche works, we will be aware of how such unfortunate phenomena work and we will do our best to stop repeating unfortunate things.

When we work through painful memories, it is important to reflect on whether we have made contracts with ourselves. Related to situations where we judge ourselves, there may be more than one contract. Then it is important to repeal the contracts after having worked with the keys. When you have worked through the painful feelings and you have discovered such a contract, you can de-program it by stating it out loud to yourself and your cells. Then all the layers of your consciousness hear what you say.

An example of making a contract with oneself

A man who consulted me had been for a charter trip to Spain where he fell in love with a lady. The man was in despair because he was married and had a family. He was so engrossed in the lady he had met that he could not let go of thinking about her. They both felt that they had met before. On the journey the group had been visiting a number of places, including a monastery. There he had strong sensations of having lived there before. When he came to me, he was determined to try a regression* to find out about what he felt. He had in fact a feeling that there was a connection between the monastery and the lady.

It turned out that he had been a monk in that particular monastery in the Middle ages. He had inner pictures where he had lived and recognized where he had walked around in despair. As a monk he lived in celibacy. Thus he had promised not to be with women sexually. It turned out that he experienced falling in love just as intensely in that life as in this. This was about 750 years ago! He hid himself away and met her secretly because he could not let go of seeing her. Simultaneously he was deeply in despair by not being able to keep the monks promise. In the regression he could see where she lived related to the monastery. A lot of feeling s came up, many of them contradiction knots and in addition a coupling between guilt and love. The relationship was discovered and he felt a tremendous shame. The strong love was connected with shame and guilt.

He discovered very soon the parallel to this life. He could see that it would help him to get clarity in his present situation if he worked through the feelings. Towards the end of the work, he became aware that he had made several agreements with himself. When he reflected on this, it turned out that the agreements influenced this life.

In the remorse of the fatal revelation he had promised himself never to have a sexual relationship with a woman which had influenced this life too. After having worked through all the feelings he had to repeal both the monks promise about living in celibacy and the contract he did with himself. He did it this way:

"I face the fact that I, in my life as a monk in the 1200s, broke the monk promise by having sex and therefore made an agreement with myself about never having sex again. I declare to all my cells that I now repeal the agreement I made with myself about not having sex. The agreement is now deleted."

You have to repeal such agreements as clearly as this example to make the particles of the soul and the cells delete what they experience as programmings. You must say it very sincerely *at least three times*. I think many people will enjoy repealing similar contracts. There are many people who have problems because of agreements made in earlier lives.

18 Self-recognition is door-opening

One of the major challenges we humans face, is self-denial. Many of us carry memories that make us run away when we are reminded about painful or unpleasant things. They are too difficult to feel and to face. The human mind is such that the things we don't want to feel we may have completely put a lid on, so that we don't remember what happened. These may be situations when we were betrayed or deceived and can be so painful that we don't manage to look back at them. There may also be situations where we acted unfavorably perhaps participating in oppression or harassment.

Maybe we once let sexual feelings become too strong so we lost control and acted in ways we don't like. These kinds of situations may cause a person to completely deny what has happened with a part of the consciousness while another part of the consciousness remembers. What is typical for such conditions is that we run away from people and situations where we have been immoral or bad. The denying part may be nice and attentive and a part that subconsciously remembers what happened, behaves badly and is in a lousy condition. It can be crabby and cranky and behave like a bully towards other people. The nice part of the person may be totally or partially in denial of what the other part of the mind is doing.

Such conditions are quite a challenge for the surroundings of these people. I can only recommend everybody to be honest with their feelings, because if you have tendencies of being violent or nasty to others, you have a problem! All human beings need to be honest with themselves. Self-denial, the way it is described here, doesn't need to last for ever. You might actually remember what you want to forget… you only want to forget all the time. It leads to an inner pressure, which in addition leads to mood changes which may give physical pain and/or depression.

An example of release of self-denial

A lady at the end of her 30s, let us call her Mary, came to me and explained that she was struggling with depressive thoughts. She was never content with herself and often she only wanted to lie down and sleep. She complained about a hip pain that would come and go and that was especially bad when she was with friends. She was also an outward person and travelled a lot. She said about herself: When I am travelling I am happy and meet many new, exciting people. Then I am seen for who I am. After a journey, however, coming back to normal life, she felt that her life became even heavier.

She often got an inner picture of someone lying in the fetal position and she wondered if it was herself. While I interview her, she said out loud: 'I wish I wasn't myself'. Such expressions that come between the lines or as sighs are often the door openers. The subconscious thoughts are rather obvious when we start observing life. Who would you have been, then? I asked. She looked at me and I could see that suddenly she was far away. The memory she needed to look at had come to the surface.

She laid down, turned away from me and started to sob loudly and said: 'I am the one who is bad. She was good and kind'. I let her cry until it silenced. Then she turned around and started to tell me about her childhood. Mary was an only child. The family was wealthy and Mary mostly got what she wanted for herself. She was independent and often home alone. Her mother was a business woman and her father travelled a lot. Sometimes they were both gone and then she stayed with a cousin. She paused before she continued about the class she had been a part of in primary school. She remembered what happened in 5th grade ... There was a girl, Alice, who came from a family of 4 children. They had a farm with sheep, cows and a horse. Alice had to help at the farm.

Alice had to help at her home and sometimes she smelled of cows. Sometimes she came too late because she had siblings she helped to kindergarten before she came to school. She was a quiet girl who always did her schoolwork. Once, the class visited Alice's family's farm. Then her classmates saw another Alice. An Alice who was accustomed to animals and who knew everything about the farm and could elegantly swing up onto her horse.

Mary cries silently. She doesn't want to say what she did. 'Everyone used to listened to me when I did things the others did not dare do... I was so tired of that girl, she was always so splendid...' The anger and the despair rises in her and then she remembers that she is here to realise her feelings so that she can set herself free from what makes her depressed.

She is determined to do it and realises what she feels about all those feelings coming up. She realizes that it was not wounds because of what someone had done to her... it was what she had done to Alice that caused the many painful feelings (guilt, shame, feelings of not being worthy of love, fear that others would accuse her and not look up to her any more).

She admits that she was the one who bullied and made the others do the same. Then she stops and it becomes quiet again. As she realised this, she understood that this was the reason she was depressed. She realised that in all the years since then, she had tried to escape from herself, much like her mother and father did in her childhood. They travelled and met new people who didn't know how they felt at home ... 'At home we were lonely all three of us. Mum was always busy talking on the phone with someone she could confide in. When Dad was at home and we were a family, we had somehow nothing to talk about. I was not good at telling them things about myself when I think about it ... I rather escaped into a book or a TV series'.

The acknowledgement became a door opener for Mary. She realised that it was because she was neither honest to herself nor to her classmates that she had the need to bully Alice. As she realised feelings coming up in her, she could see how the loneliness and the feeling of being disregarded made her come up with stories to cover how she really felt as a child.

It was quiet for a long time. Suddenly she exclaimed: 'I haven't lived my life'! What do you mean? I asked. 'I haven't done what I really wanted to do because I lied so much that I had to fulfil a picture of myself that wasn't true. I had to fit in everybody else's perception of me'.

A waterfall of words and tears gushed out of Mary that day. She visualised Alice ahead of her and begged her for forgiveness and felt that she came to her and said OK. When she had finished, she was physically exhausted, but happy. She had managed to forgive herself for much of what she had done. She got a long time to herself after the counselling. She asked for pen and paper because she wanted to write down the things she realised. She wanted to make new decisions for her life and she wanted to write them down. One of the things she decided was to write in her diary. 'I know it will help me to be honest with myself', she said.

'This is the most important day in my life', she said when she left. It has been tough, but now I know that I can wind up every thread and I will dare to stand face to face with myself. This is the loveliest thing I have ever done. I'm not afraid of anything when I see that I have managed to get through this.

19 How to find the memory?

The everyday feelings

I recommend starting by observing your life. Start noticing when you get irritated, disappointed, sorry, when you get a guilty conscience or feel that others are better than you. Everyday such feelings are activated in some form in us. When you get time to yourself, try as best you can, to put into words exactly how you feel. Through such simple means you are about to get a direct connection between your soul and your mind. You immediately get new insights. If memories show up, they are important to take a look at. There may be things muttering just under the surface of your mind. Unless you are aware that the muttering slows your life energy, you might not notice but such muttering can turn out to be something you have suppressed for a long time and got used to. As you get used to observing your life, it becomes easier and easier to recognize what you actually feel. It is, to a large degree, possible to remember memories on our own. All the following techniques may lead you to finding memories and associated feelings.

The list of where the different feelings are stuck in the body

When you observe your feelings through your everyday life, please notice simultaneously if pain and sensations occur in the body. If you have chronic pain or pain coming and going; know that they are related to oppressed feelings. Take a look at the listing further ahead in the book of how feelings prevent life energy. Perhaps you find that your pain is similar to what is listed there? Maybe you realize what it might be by reading the listing? Your feelings may be similar. It is important that you don't use the list too literary, but let it show the direction of the work within yourself. When you start realising what you feel, you can try out many different ways to put into words what you feel. Two words that resemble each other may have completely different effects. You feel it right through when it fits!

Regression – to travel back in time

If you want to work on certain feelings or a certain situation that made you react emotionally, you can do this in the following way: Make the intention to take a look at what you struggle about. Then, let go of it, so that you don't create expectations. You can read the following relaxing exercise on an audio track or you can let someone read it for you. – You can also read it thoroughly and remember how to do it.

Relaxing exercise and introduction to regression

Lie down in a pleasant place where you can be alone. Close your eyes and relax by taking a deep breath three times. With each breath, feel that you are letting go more and more of tensions in the body. Move your thought to your toes. Imagine that you let go of them – that they simply lie there. Move your thought on to your feet and imagine that you let go of them. Relax completely in your ankles – calves – knees – thighs. Take your time. Imagine that you let go of both legs and let them lie on the substrate. Let go of all tension in your hips and your abdomen in the same way. Observe the breathing going in and out and feel that you let go of all tension in your stomach and your chest. Let your thoughts wander upwards through all the muscles in your entire back, until you reach your neck and feel that your back is entirely relaxed. Use plenty of time.

Then move your thought to your fingers. Feel that you let go of them so that they just lie there and relax. Move on to the hands, hand joints, forearms, elbows, upper arms, shoulders. Take your time. Now you feel that the throat gets in the same totally relaxed condition...the jaw, mouth, cheek, eyes, forehead...the whole face is now totally relaxed. Then move the thought to the back of your neck and let it wander up the entire scalp until you are at the top of your head. Your entire body is now totally relaxed. Now you move your thought to the middle of the chest and ask your soul to show you what you need to look at.

If a memory occurs, your will probably recognize that the memory is about the same kind of feelings that you asked to see the roots of at the beginning of the exercise. Most likely you will soon recognize it as a parallel event. As it produces new feelings when you realise, you might get up several situations containing the same pattern. Look at them and see the connections, but continue to work in the memory that you were shown first, until you have forgiven and have let go of the pain. Many times the pain in the other situations dissolves up by itself when you understand what they are all about. Your soul sees and understands that it does not serve you to carry them. You can optionally work with them on a later occasion.

If you don't get forth memories or happenings at once, take time. This is about letting go of the mind's rational thoughts and getting beyond, to your feelings. Just be present and let go of all expectations. If you don't get forth anything, you can for example imagine that you are standing by a big curtain. When you take a look through a hole in the curtain, you see something you need to find out about your life. Then you can move the curtain aside and discover more and more of what you want to see. You can also imagine that the curtain that prevents you can be opened in several ways. Use your imagination! For instance, imagine that you have a knife in your hand so that you can cut a hole in it. Make a split down to the floor so that your body can go through it... and suddenly you are where you need to be.

If it is completely dark when you have achieved a relaxed condition, you can imagine that you have a torch enabling you to spread light onto what you need to see. Choose spontaneously! If you don't get pictures, start realizing what you feel and more feelings come flowing! Sometime you don't get up places or times.

To travel into the pain by the help of the thoughts

On my way to finding these keys I was inspired by a method that the American author Brandon Bays* describes in her book 'The journey'. It explains about how you can travel by the help of the thought into the pain in the body to find answers. Our cells are conscious and have all the information we need. They signalize to our mind with the nervous system by giving us physical pain, if there is something not in alignment with the life energy. The energy of the soul is present in every single cell. I do it this way: I let my thought move directly to the painful place and ask the cells there to tell me what they say. They literary repeat exactly the pain of the soul. Be in the pain point by your thought and wait for answers! You may get words, pictures, moods, phrases, etc. You can also get the feeling this is about. If you get a feeling, simply start realising what you feel! The memory can come forth completely clearly because you remember it from this life. It is transported to your mind by the energy system! It may be deeply hidden so it takes time to understand what comes forth.

You may simply get a strong feeling when you seek things with the help of your thought. Get started and realize that what you feel and what happens is that the memory gets stronger! The feelings come flowing and you are realising! It may be a memory you cannot remember. Then there may be pieces; sensations or words. Know that what you feel is always right, so start to realise what you feel. If you bring to your memory the feelings from your everyday situation that made you search, they will help you show the way. When you move into your cells this way, you may get a surprise because many people carry memories that they don't want to face. It may be something you have repressed completely because it was too painful to see and feel, but it may also belong to someone else so that you carry someone else's pain because you pitied them. Your cells can get forth memories all the way back to the fetal stage. Some people have experienced it as traumatic to be born, so in some cases, birth itself may be a memory coming forth.

You can also get up scenes that you immediately know you haven't experienced in this life. It seems that some people have to experience that they have lived past lives before they accept that our souls live many lives. If you experience going into such pictures and discover how the incident and the emotions influence choices and actions in this life – then you no longer have any doubt!

Our souls have another perception of time than our minds, so when you travel back to a memory, you may experience being there. Your soul doesn't manage to let go of what happened unless you are willing to realise what you felt at that time. Earlier lives can be experienced just as real as memories you remember from this life. Your feelings are real the way they were at the time when it happened. You soon discover parallels to this life.

Regressions may go very far back in time. The feelings in the present may have ancient roots. They may even come from cultures that we don't know today. Yet it is the feeling you need to acknowledge and release. The sensation that the memory gives, is an indication of whether it is old. For instance I have experienced leading a regression where the client was in a situation where she had to sacrifice her child. As a memory this had a major impact on her present life, but an act that is unthinkable in our society.

When you are in a regression, you are present with your conscious I, at the same time as you can experience being in another world. There are therapists who offer regression and getting help to go back across time and space can be a door opener for many. If you get someone to help you that does not help you to process feelings, I warmly recommend that you relate to your feelings in memory and use the techniques described here. There are also other similar techniques.

Album

A nice method that I highly recommend for those who want to work steadily with themselves to improve their life quality, is to use a technique I call 'memory photo album'. Before you begin, say to yourself that you want to find a memory that is important to you, related to where you are right now in life. Then, sit down in a comfortable position, take some deep breaths and relax well each time you exhale. Close your eyes! When you feel relaxed, imagine that you have an album of your life in front of you. See your name, birthplace and your date of birth on the outside. Your life album. This needs to be characterized by who you are. Imagine that the album contains all the episodes that you need to look at throughout your life. These should also be good memories that make you appreciate yourself and see how great you are! Your soul will lead you to what you need to look at first, then when you open it, you may already at the first page pop up a memory that you know is important. Then you only need to go straight into the picture! You may decide to start with early childhood and look at the pictures one by one as they show up on the pages in your album.

An alternative method is to sit down and look through the paper photos from your childhood, having the same purpose. Most people have either picture boxes or albums. Then good memories, and sometimes less good memories, show up. Allow yourself to feel the good feelings too! When you come across a memory that needs to be worked through, you will know it immediately.

Pendulum

Many people may wonder at how we can find answers by using a pendulum. That's probably because we are so accustomed to thinking of the physical reality as the only real. As a pendulum you can use a piece of jewelry that you attach at one end of a chain or a pendulum made for the purpose. Make sure the pendulum is for your own personal use. Maybe you find this too mysterious? I have found that it is the particles' ability of awareness and communication that makes it possible. Even the light that surrounds us is created by particles, which are connected to other particles.

It's not always easy for everyone to make the pendulum work, but don't give up at the first attempt. It can be a very good tool. You also need to work on yourself if you doubt the pendulum because your perception can influence it. You need to liberate the mind and await answers. You can conveniently make it a habit to say: I am… your name, birth date and birthplace before you begin. It will help your cells to find clear answers for you. (As you become accustomed to using the pendulum, check sometimes whether there is any energy not being your own that might mislead you in your energy field. Sometimes it happens.)

You can ask questions to the pendulum by holding the chain firmly by your hand and then wait for answers by the pendulum's swing. If you call on the consciousness of your body, your cells can give you very exact answers, even about things that happened far away and a long time ago… if your soul has experienced it, you can find answers.

How to do it: Hold the pendulum steady and let it hang at rest. Ask your soul, or your cell consciousness to show by the pendulum how it responds 'yes'. Then, how it responds 'no' and then how it responds 'will not / can not answer'. Once you've got three different signals that way, you can begin. (It may swing rightwards, leftwards, back and forth in two ways.) When it will not respond, it may be a good reason. Maybe you already know what you ask for? Perhaps there is no clear answer. Practicing intuition is important!

If you feel overrun and wounded after a day at work and you want to find out whether your feelings may be rooted in the past, you can bring forth the pendulum when you get home. Once you have made contact, ask for examples: Do these emotions have roots in my childhood? Do you get 'yes', ask: Do they have roots from before I started school? Getting 'No', you may ask: Was I older than six? Do you get 'Will not answer', it may have happened when you were six years! The pendulum can bring you exactly into the memory. As you get used to this, your own intuition gives you questions. Be true to your feelings and ask about what comes to you! Suddenly you remember a happening that gave you exactly the same feelings as today, and then you have got started!

If it doesn't work that easily, don't give up of that reason. Keep the emotions that were triggered earlier during the day as starting points for the questions. Maybe you get 'no' when asking whether it was from your childhood. Then you can ask: Did it happen in my teens? Was I an adult? You may get yes to both answers so follow your intuition, your feelings and any pain in your body when you go on. You may ask: Did it concern school? The pupils? My parents? My siblings? Relate your questions to where you lived, to parts of your life at that time. If you remember the memory, it will come to you. If not, continue to ask until you are able to imagine the situation that fits your feelings. If you have put a lid on it, feel what feels right and admit what you feel. The very most important thing is to feel whether the answers are right for you and start using the Keys of liberation. If the answers don't fit your feelings, go back after some time and ask again. Follow impulses coming to you in the meantime.

If you get 'no' to all the questions whether it happened in this life, ask then: Do these feelings have roots in a former life? If you get yes, you face an exciting journey of exploration. Ask: Was I the same gender as I am now? Did it happen in my country? Did it happen in Europe? Did it happen AC or BC? Was I rich? Was I married? And so on. Let the situations that triggered your feelings contribute to guiding you to what to ask about! A very relevant question: Is there anyone in the memory that I know in this life? The feelings in the situation resemble what happened this particular day, so you bring your feelings from the present into a timeframe and experience what may be from the middle ages, or may be from a previous century. Like before: Realise exactly what you feel and the doors start to open.

20 Grief and how to relate to grief

One thing is certain. Our soul needs comfort and rest. Our soul needs to grieve. Allowing this is being true to our feelings. Still, we have the ability to leave behind most kinds of pain when we have a distance to it. All painful experiences actually need distance and processing before you can apply the Keys. It feels as if the soul needs to get back the normal condition to be able to look back at things. In some cases, a few months are enough. When it comes to deaths, accidents, family splits, a breakup with a partner, events that have made a profound influence, I recommend that the grief process takes a year.

Anniversaries and holidays we remember and then we are reminded. After the first year is gone, however, it is time to begin to release the grief and loss. If it was an accident, many emotions need to be released. Maybe there were other situations associated with what happened that are important to look at. As I see it, it is an important feature of life when we lose someone we love, whether by divorce or death: We must learn to deal with the grief so that we can live on and find life joy and a meaningful life.

Those who die, go on living in ethereal bodies in an ethereal dimension. Take a look at the spinning pattern at page … The particles there spin in other patterns than in atoms. The ethereal world is just as real, just different from the physical. If you are a person who doubts that there is life after death, I encourage you to search for books telling you about life after death, so that you can read about others' experiences beyond. Such an understanding may help you get a much more relaxed relation to your own life. Gradually I have achieved contact with many souls in the ethereal dimension and I know that the soul leaves the physical existence in an ethereal body, a kind of invisible copy of the physical body that exists in the same "space". When people die, they experience being themselves creating and moving by the help of their thought. They can communicate both by words and thoughts. They have the ability to communicate with us inside our energy fields, by being close to us. We need to learn more about human nature so that we understand that dead people can present thoughts in our energy field. Then we perceive their thoughts as if they are our own. However, when we understand that it's the dead people's opportunity to communicate with us, we may open up to interpreting impulses coming to us in several ways. Sometimes, the people in the ethereal dimension help us to see things we need to see. Other times they communicate how they are where they are. In this way we are actually given impulses from those who are dead, and humans who are open for it can see their face by their inner eye and communicate with them.

When we feel that the grief period is over, it's time to use the Keys. They work as fine tools for that. Those who have experienced loosing someone may become surprised by what kind of feelings they have related to the dead person. Again, you need to be honest with yourself, because your pain and subconscious thoughts may contribute to pulling down the person who died. You need to release their part also. There may be situations back in time and there may be feelings related to the dying situation. It is not uncommon that the person who grieves feels anger towards the dead person. This may have several reasons, but the anger often has roots in a feeling of having been let down. The soul may have quite another perception than the mind because the soul may have communicated directly with the soul of the person who died without understanding why he or she had to leave. The anger may have its roots in something that happened long before the person died and thus it is important to work through situations from earlier years.

When you have lost someone who has wandered to the other side, it is important to understand that your thoughts about them influence them. It means, that if your grief for example means that what happened is not possible to let go of, you hold them in your perception about what happened. Your grief, despair and maybe hatred towards the person(s) that caused their death, influences them and pulls them down. This is the reason I strongly recommend working through the grief when a year has passed and, as much as you can, leave the pain behind you. This is also one of the reasons that I recommend you find certainty where there is life after death. Saying 'Rest in peace' to someone who has died, I do not recommend. Human souls who have died do rest a while if they have been ill, but then they are shown how they can create their own homes and their own lives, even how they can look back at situations in life that they can work through, release and learn from.

Many who have experienced losing their dear ones continue to communicate with them after they are dead. They feel their presence and speak to them as if they are present. This is natural during the first period after someone had died. It's common that people who die are around their closest family until the funeral. However, it is actually necessary to ask oneself whether one begrudges the other to live their own lives by their own choices and their own friends on the other side. Afterlife is manifold and rich for human souls that set themselves free from the grief of dying. They find joy and community in the ethereal dimension. If we believe that they are in our physical surroundings and speak to them as if they are here all the time, they will feel obliged to be here to comfort us. It serves neither them nor us in the long run. By my knowledge of life after death, I know that humans who pass over get new friends and create their own new lives. For that reason it is important to work through the grief. However, it doesn't mean that those who are dead forget their family and friends who live in a physical body, if they experience their life as good. They then 'come visiting' by their own will now and then by imagining that they are in the rooms where their closest family and friends live. Then they are there, in the same space as their dear ones, just subtle and invisible to the physical eyes, but able to communicate with their souls.

(After what I have learned about the soul level of humans, I have discovered that evil energies/particles actually exist and that they can occupy humans and do evil acts. If a person who has done something awful to you asks for forgiveness, or says that he or she doesn't remember it or cannot understand that they have done it, I recommend that you give that person a chance. They might have been ruled over by such a dark energy. In some cases humans become really evil and say things about themselves and that what they did was right. Follow your heart. What I can suggest for those of you who one way or another have been in contact with such evil people; try to release your feelings as well as you can, and neutralise yourself in relation to the person, so that he or she becomes a no-person. Sooner or later I know those people actually perish because the particles dissolve them when they die.)

21 Practical use of the Keys of Liberation

It's a good idea to start using the Keys when negative feelings show up in your everyday life. This may be a challenge, but believe me, it's the best door opener. Yes, sometimes you are angry for a reason! You are allowed to be angry and it is actually healthy! The challenge is finding out whether the situation occurred because of old emotional baggage or not. Realise that your feelings are your own, only! Know, that your wounds and your subconscious thoughts may have contributed to creating the situation so that you can find what is hidden inside of you. This is a new way of relating to life, so spend time finding out! To start with it may seem that what you need to do is to turn things upside down. Try to see it as a sport, a competition with yourself. It may be a situation at your work place, a conflict in the family, or simply unpleasant thoughts, feelings or physical pain that keep returning. Working to release feelings is incredibly exciting. You are not going to be bored!

You can see it this way; things happening to you in your external life reveal your inner landscape. Try to see people that trigger your feelings so that you get angry or wounded as gifts to you along your path, rather than letting your anger overflow towards them. Stop and think! Did they mean to hurt me? Did they want to make me angry? What is it by their statements or ways of acting that make me angry? Does this resemble something I have experienced before? If so, try to calm down and find a place where you can be alone. I know that this isn't easy. But if you later discover that the person didn't have any intention of making you angry, but that your anger had its roots in your own past, you can choose to go back to the person to apologise. Then you can turn the situation to a positive happening. Sometimes we meet people who fit into our own patterns.

How can you know what is created by your own patterns and what is created by someone else's? It is when you react by emotional pain that you have the reason to relate to your feelings and feel them, really face them. Sometimes there can be a reason for others to be justly angry at you?

When you realise exactly what you feel, it sometimes feels as if you 'twist the knife in the wound' so that it bleeds. It is as if the wound is being cleansed. You need to empty yourself of pain. The imprisoned feelings must come up to the surface. Let your tears flow. It is really healthy to cry, it feels like a dam is bursting and it has to flow until it's empty. Put all your feelings into words as they come to mind. I recommend always saying them out loud to yourself. It is important to try out sentences until you feel that the words hit the feelings.

Some types of feelings are very strong in the physical body. We can be compared with pressure cookers that need to release steam. Usually anger, despair, bitterness and hatred are kinds of feelings we need to get out in physical ways. It works well to use our arms to beat something to get them out. Usually I lie down when I release pain, but when I get up strong anger, it is useful to sit on my knees and bang my fists in the sofa or bed to get out the suppressed aggression. You need to express your feelings simultaneously. Many years ago when attending a psychodrama group, we used a carpet beater on a foam mattress to get out aggression and I witnessed many examples of how important this is. I can remember that in the first experimental phase of release work I walked on the shoreline and cried out in the wind and waves. You can find your way to express strong feelings. Beating rugs is an excellent way if you live where no one can hear you! Because you have to use your voice when you do it! The important thing is to recognise what we actually feel angry about because our culture has for so long led us to keep feelings inside.

When you are by yourself and have calmed down, you can sit / lie down, close your eyes and feel the painful feelings. Feel what you feel and say it out loud to yourself: I realize that I feel ... and be very specific. Admit everything exactly the way you feel it, even though it may be an ugly word. That is why you need to be alone. You need to get it out! Say it in many ways and you'll discover that some words hit better than others. Be honest with yourself and do this thoroughly, relating to everything you feel about the situation that arose. When you sit or lie down to do this, several more emotions usually emerge. They come to the surface when you give time to feel them. Then they may start to dissolve. Sometimes it can work well to express your feelings to clarify the situation and you realize that what happened occurred because of the other people's manners.

When you begin to realise that you feel, you may start getting pictures of memories. Suddenly you remember a painful childhood memory emotionally. You may remember parallels to the event. Travel back to the memory, be present as the person you were at that time and work consistently through all the emotions with all four keys. Be in the first memory that pops up, it is probably the most important. Usually great insight and inner release follows. You may want to write down the other memories that you remember and work through them later. You will then see them in the light of the first incident.

In a release situation, you must expect to put into words very strong feelings towards people that you actually love. It is absolutely necessary to take them out when you are on your own. Then you get a lot better relationship to the people concerned afterwards. Remember that no one needs to be perfect. We need to allow ourselves and others to do wrong steps and to do the best we can to forgive each other.

If there is no memory coming but you still have the same feelings without being able to let go of them, you can use a pendulum*. Bring the feelings from earlier that day and ask for help. Use your intuition.

Maybe you have pain in your body also? Take a look at the list of where the different feelings are stuck in the body as it can give you a hint in which direction you need to look. Lie and relax for a while and move your thoughts into the pain and ask your cells what they can tell you. This can be effective. Be prepared release work can be very painful to experience but know that it is the loveliest feeling there is when you have acknowledged the pain and managed to forgive.

Be present in the memory and realize what you feel by saying the sentences loud. This works the best. Remember, it's the feelings you need to acknowledge, not the situation. The more profound, the better it is. Do not only say the feeling but why you feel the way you feel. Is there anything you denied to see because it was too painful? Because you did something stupid?

Be honest with yourself!

An example from a client who got up a school situation from 2. Grade

I realise that I feel that the others are much better than me.
I realise that I feel that I am not good enough in others eyes.
I realise that I feel that I am ashamed because I am not making it.
I realise that I feel that I am afraid that the others think I am stupid.
I realise that I feel that the teacher doesn't see me.
I realise that I feel sad because I feel that the others don't care about me because they think I am stupid.

We need to be as detailed as this! Something worth noticing: It is the way we interpret a situation that makes us feel the way we do. We interpret all situations related to those wounds we have in our baggage already. It is no guarantee that the others feel the same as we feel. That is why we need to release our own feelings!

You can replace the word realise with similar words that feel better for you, for example, admit, accept, acknowledge. This is a very important part of this method because by recognising and facing what you actually feel, you break the tendency to suppress the pain. It is not enough to only express what you feel. It is the recognising word that make your soul start releasing.

Say things in different ways until you hit the feeling and repeat the phrase until you feel that the feeling fades. When it is very painful, find out if there is a Gordian knot*! If it is very painful so that you cannot stop crying, take a break and let your soul work on her/his own for a while. You calm down, and when you come back to the situation the worst pain may have left.

Many feelings can be quite complicated, so take your time. The sentences can get 2 and 3 parts, for instance: I realise that I feel a deep grief because I feel unworthy because he violated me. Or – I realise that I feel ashamed that I was not able to take responsibility because it's always taken away from me. All variations of emotion are hidden within us. When you feel that you have emptied yourself, when it calms down, you can move on to the forgiveness phase. In many cases it is primarily yourself you need to forgive. Most of us are struggling, being too self-critical. Our culture has not taught us that we need to care for ourselves in a balanced manner. Feel and reflect. Be in the memory while working with forgiveness. At the same time, bring the adult, sensible person you are.

If you choose "the inner child technique", close your eyes and see yourself in your imagination from outside at the place where the event happened. You can do this related to situations that happened recently too. Sit down with yourself. Remove the people that were there and imagine a bench or chair to sit on, unless it is there already. Hold your arms around the one you were then. This works. Be fully present in the present at the time when it happened. Speak in the present tense. Give comfort and warmth to yourself. Such a situation is experienced as totally real and many experience remembering details, even smell from the situation. Now you can apply you-form and say (the example from school):

I forgive you… your name… for feeling that the others are much better that you.
I forgive you… for feeling that that you are not good enough in their eyes.
I forgive you… that you feel ashamed for not making it.
I forgive you… for being afraid that the others think you are stupid.
I forgive you… that you feel that the teacher doesn't see you.
I forgive you… that you feel sad because you feel that the others don't care about you because they think you are stupid.

To say to yourself that you forgive what feels painful at that time works usually much stronger than saying to yourself: "I forgive myself for what I feel". If you in this position want to cry, you need to go back to the first key and realise whatever comes up. When you see yourself from outside, your empathy with yourself at the time when this happened awakens. You see new angles. That will make you get into the depth of your feelings. I deeply recommend doing this. It is really what heals the wounds of the soul.

Then bring the people into the memory one by one, be in the feelings from that time and tell them exactly what you feel. Think through, if what they did to you was because of lack of insights and understanding? Do you think they meant to be bad? Maybe you can tell them that you forgive them, because you see that they carry their own baggage from their childhood, and that you understand that they too have wounds that made them do what they did. Ask for forgiveness and explain why you did what you did, if that is necessary for the situation. Make sure you don't blame as this suggests a need to place guilt outside of you. If you feel the need to blame, you need to go back and realise that you feel the need to blame ... and forgive yourself for it.

When the forgiveness phase is over, you can continue by giving love to yourself in the same position. It is natural to give love and comfort to the one you were then, all the time along the way. Often it's what you need the very most, so I recommend that you mix love into the forgiveness key when it's about very painful feelings.

It is important to get through with a natural love for yourself. This is because you have denied it when life was too difficult to deal with. Therefore I recommend that you use the love key just as thoroughly as in the other phases. The phrases become a transformation of what has been hurt. Your mind, which manages "the caregiver" who you are for yourself, can do this in two ways. Whether you talk to yourself outside yourself, as shown above, or you say it like this:

I love myself, although I feel that the others are much better than me.
I love myself, although I feel that I'm not good enough in their eyes.
I love myself, although I feel that I am ashamed because I don't make it.
I love myself, although I am afraid that the others think I'm stupid.
I love myself, although I feel that the teacher don't see me.
I love myself, although I feel sad because I feel that the others don't care about me because they think I'm stupid.

The let-go phase is important because then you reflect on whether you feel that you have left behind what was painful. The work with your feelings will give you insights in what unwanted thinking- and acting patterns have led to in your life. Here too, I recommend working consistently:

I now let go of feeling the others are much better than me.
I now let go of feeling that I'm not good enough in their eyes.

I now let go of the feeling that I am ashamed because I don't make it.
I now let go of being afraid that others think I'm stupid.
I now let go of feeling that the teacher did not see me.
I now let go that I feel sad because I feel that the others don't care about me because they think I'm stupid.

In addition, after having ended the key work, when you lie down to rest and feel well, you can repeat to yourself: «I am made of love. I am love. I am life joy. I am proud to be who I am as myself». By that you give a great gift to yourself and to your cells.

If you observe yourself in the time to come, you may discover that you have more memories of a similar nature. Usually it is not enough to work through only one memory to get rid of what we struggle with. Be an optimist, because now you have started to learn how your psyche works. Know that making journeys inside yourself is more exciting than any detective story! Usually tears flow during a release work. It feels good. A lovely, relaxed feeling spreads throughout the body afterwards. After a release work, it is important to rest and know that you appreciate your body.

22 Going on

Scientific method requires inter alia referring to what theorists have researched and proven earlier. When someone comes from the sideline with completely new, fresh thoughts they have until now been met with strong opposition in academic environments. I have experienced that my thoughts about particles were rejected because the article was not written in line with academic tradition. It contained no references and the language was too informal. I wonder about this. Are people in higher education and research afraid that someone with a "simpler" background might know something that they don't know? Could there be other ways to acquire knowledge than through the education system?

It puzzles me that medical research mainly seems to be based on guidelines that were drawn up long before atomic and quantum physics were born. It focuses, as I understand it from the patient's position, on finding external causes of diseases. Could this be the reason why many doctors fail to help their patients with anything other than medicine?

Pain is in every sense real, although it is a subjective experiences for the individual. It may not be measurable the way old scientific research rules require, but I think it is certainly possible to do research on pain sensations. If we combine a qualitative* method where we do interviews and observe, with quantitative* method, where we collect data and compare cases, we will over time, and with groups of patients, find coincident answer.

Actually I mean that one should treat patients unless they learn and make experiences about how our feelings influence their body. I think all kinds of healthcare professionals should work with themselves and learn how to release their own emotional baggage as a part of their education. To learn what emotional wounds lead to, can only be truly understood by our own experience. Then you get insights in general human nature. I mean that it is very important to understand that the teaching about this ought to be experiential learning. To really get good insights at the level we except from medical doctors and psychologists, cannot be learnt only through lectures and reading books. I suggest that those who treat humans within health care, in the future should have a new type of preparatory course in understanding themselves and how to release their own emotional pain.

I mean that research in the future must be based upon cells' consciousness. The way I experience it, there is an enormous knowledge about life in human cells. In every single cell are actually the programmings that make a human being a human being. In addition in many human beings there is much knowledge about the human history from the soul's angle, which can give valuable information to our society today. We can find the old wisdom about the origin of humanity. Many people on earth carry memories about earlier lives far back in time. Their cells can give just as interesting information as excavations and old scriptures when cell consciousness becomes an accepted understanding. Maybe archeologists one day will start getting educated in exploring history by regressions? I can tell a whole lot about old Egypt that Egyptologists don't know, things that can help them interpret hieroglyphs and pictures.

In Norway we express it such when someone is ill, for example: 'She has got arthritis'. Or 'He has got asthma'. It seems as if there is a perception among most people that we get illness and pain by coincidence. As if they come flying with the wind. Many people go to the doctor expecting that he or she will make them healthy. It seems as if the doctors and the health care have responsibility for our health. We put our lives in their hands. This is not the way it should to be. Every one of us has the responsibility – both in taking care of our health – and in finding out how we can contribute to get well when we get ill. A huge change of attitude is needed.

In this book I have limited what I have written to pain in the body. I have not discussed diseases. In many cases I am certain that diseases are caused by emotions that are being repeated the way described here. I have no doubt about that. It is a complex area that I want to do further research on. I have also come across several cases that are not due to feelings, but are caused by dysfunctional particles. I am happy to be at disposal of researchers who wish to corroborate and explore the allegations I put forward in this this book.

I think it is possible to develop a teaching program so that everybody can see that they are able to take responsibility for their health to a much larger extent. To reduce the heath queues and budgets, most people need to get insights in how the feelings influence the body. I hope the knowledge I bring will make possible a new health policy to grow forth. I would appreciate attending universities and colleges to lecture on my experiences and findings.

23 The good life

We humans are physical beings living in a body but are at the same time multi-dimensional, non-linear beings that exist across time and space. This is what is so fantastic about being human. We really need to learn to appreciate life in new ways, to be humble and at the same time proud of who we are.

The very greatest challenge is how we use our free will, the essence of life itself. Life energy allows us to choose how we want to dispose of the gift of life. It leaves the responsibility to us. To you and me. It means that we are fully responsible for all the choices in life. We tend to push responsibility on to our parents, employers, authorities, the school, the doctor, the hospital. When you reflect deeply, you know the answer for you and your life.

It is when we are willing to see, to admit and to be honest with ourselves, that we really achieve life moving forward but by what measurement? The answer is in life quality. If you dare to admit that you have done a mistake, you grow! Then joy of life and new discoveries about yourself come in its wake. You learn to forgive yourself so that you don't take yourself so seriously. Then you can use the blank sheets lying in front of you in new ways. When we learn to forgive and let go, life changes dramatically.

Our choices decide what direction life takes. Do you let others' opinion decide over you? Do you make choices that are not really your own? In the society of our time we are constantly bombarded by impressions from media, commercials, Internet and public debates with strong meanings. In addition many people around us are keen on being slim, beautiful and successful. How do we find our own opinion and what we stand for in the middle of this? My experience is that we feel it in the heart when we are alone and when we ask ourselves what we really want to do. When you find the right answer for you, you too will find inner peace.

Do you think it is OK to work around the truth a little, so you outwardly retain your face while you feel bleak inside? Losing face is a very painful experience. If you stand for your truth, if you are honest and apologise when you do mistakes, you grow both in your own eyes and in those of others. To actively choose to live by good values is a choice I recommend warmly. You can choose to make positive agreements with yourself. Being honest, for example, what does this actually mean? What about keeping promises to yourself and to others?

Gradually an insight that I gladly share grew forth in me: We all have the free will to dispose of the life energy by the choices we do. Not only the big choices, but also the minor choices we do in our daily lives. What we choose to say and what we don't say. Whether we choose to be generous or we choose to be greedy, whether we choose to be sociable or dismissive. Whether we choose to be honest or if it is OK to avoid the truth and make our own truth? Whether we choose to participate actively in what we do or just float along? Whether we choose to be grateful or we take for granted what comes our way? Whether we choose to be considerate or we act without concern for others?

Think about how you use your days. Do you slop down in front of your TV or can you find more joy if you participate in a choir or play pool with your friends? Is it more important to follow that certain series on TV than to join a community, to do theatre or voluntary work? Such choices are actually very important when it comes to our life energy and to have an active relationship to life. What I have found as important, is to choose to do what gives joy. or to decide to enjoy what you need to do!

I mean that we are here on Earth both to develop as individuals and to develop in community with others. Our choices in life create what we experience. What we see around us at a global level in the world shows the values that humanity has created all-together. The world today sadly reflects spiritual decay and things are looking rather miserable at the moment, in my opinion. All our collective choices create the societies we live in. What is important, is to find out what good choices are, so that we move in a direction that serves both ourselves, people around us, nature and the entire earth and the global society. I mean we influence just as much with the small choices in our daily lives, as when we vote in elections. It's because attitudes create trends and directions in society and a way of being is contagious, moving from one human being to the next. When you know that emotional baggage limits the ability to see solutions and possibilities, it isn't difficult to see that active release work will lead to a better world. Maybe the human beings who are eager to release their emotional pain will be those who show the way to a new world order?

What's the point in releasing old memories of the past if I am healthy and fit in all ways you might ask. It is not only influencing your personal life, but all the people you meet and all the challenges you will face through your life. All human beings have wounds to a greater or lesser degree. Perhaps, when you know the psychological mechanisms and how they affect your life, you will want to remove what prevents you from seeing new solutions? In addition, by releasing you will be an example for people around you to do the same.

One of the driving forces when releasing my emotional baggage was the certainty that I one day would be able to create a good and meaningful life without obstacles. I understood that the limiting thoughts in my subconscious prevented me from fulfilling my dreams. It is such thoughts that prevent us from believing in ourselves, from finding the right answers and from seeing the possibilities lying right in front of us. They also prevent the right people from coming our way. However, when we remove limiting, subconscious thoughts, we grow as human beings and we are able optimistically to see and experience possibilities we never saw previously.

Doing things differently requires willpower. It is necessary to find it inside of us, when facing heavy, difficult challenges. When we experience how wonderful we feel after having worked through something very painful, we have the driving force to work more.

One thing is certain: We don't find answers unless we are willing to stop and ask ourselves questions. There are a number of factors that make you who you are! You are unique. Only you can find answers to what is right for you. Only you can find your own strength. You have the rights and all the answers in your life. You can ask yourself: Is this the way I want life to be? Am I the one making the decisions in my life? As you release, you get connected with your Self, the center of your soul, which means that your soul increasingly gets the same understanding. Eventually you will feel exactly what is right for you and you will feel safe and confident in all situations. As this happens, the reach of your energy field will increase and so will the connection to universal consciousness, which means that ideas and solutions will come easily to you.

It is our own limiting perception about ourselves that keeps us stuck. If you have thoughts about yourself that you are not good enough, then you aren't! If you, on the contrary have the perception about yourself that you are great, significant and co-creating in society, you are already on your way to being that. The perceptions about ourselves are of enormous significance. This is the reason self-appreciation is a part of this path. True love for oneself is first of all to accept oneself the way we are and at the same time see how important it is to accept and love others where they are on the their path.

From early childhood we learn that it is selfish to focus on oneself. Maybe this is the reason many people avoid self-development? Now when you read this book, you can see that it is not particularly selfish, but rather requires honesty, willingness, determination and perseverance. The truth is; it is our wounds that cause us to be selfish. It is when we feel that we don't have enough that we become greedy. It is when we feel that we are not seen, that we need to be seen in many different ways ... either by being rude or by making others pity us. It's the things we don't want to see that make our ego grow.

There are signs in the collective consciousness that there is going to be a change in the feeling of responsibility in the years to come. Humans have for a long time been looking for new answers, for different models for life. To discover that we are responsible for ourselves and our lives the way I suggest here may, I think, may be a challenge for many people. I observe that several people I know simply place their lives in the hands of doctors and the health services, thinking they will put them in good shape. It's hard to face the fact that one's illness or physical pain is caused by oneself. The fact is; it is the ways we are thinking about our bodies that have prevented us from knowing how we can take care of ourselves.

My experience with the coltsfoot made me ponder on the nature of the soul for many years. This is what I have discovered since: When I experienced being the coltsfoot, it was because the soul energy has an ability to be both very tiny – and enormously big. Our soul has the ability to vibrate and propagate its vibration so that it fills a 'space'. That is the nature of the soul. I was inside the coltsfoot as if I was my soul. The coltsfoot showed me the true nature of life energy, the way it exists in the plant kingdom. It hasn't any soul, but must contain a similar energy that I characterize as self pride and joy. The way I experienced the coltsfoot, I think is the core of life energy in everything alive. Love, pride and joy.

If you think the contents of this book is a challenge, take your time and let it sink in. If you read it again after some time, you will discover that things have fallen into place for you. Good luck!

Explanations of terms and information about names that are marked with an asterisk

***Affirmations** are confirming, positive sentences that we repeat to manifest what we want to happen in life. This is based upon the principle that thoughts are creating. When we in addition visualize what we wish for, having a clear intention about it, repeating sentences that confirm it, it will manifest, according many books. Page...

***Anxiety** is a strong irrational feeling of fear that you cannot control. It is an irrational feeling that may occur suddenly. Physically you may experience increased heartbeat, breathing problems, stomach pain. Page...

***Archetypical patterns** I call these thought patterns that I have found in almost all human beings. They have their roots from our soul's origin. I have found them by releasing lives far back in time. They form several ways of reacting that most people would call human. I am certain that it's possible to release them. This usually brings great insights in one's psyche. Page...

***Brandon Bays** is an American writer, facilitator and lecturer. The book "The journey" (1999) is known all over the world and contains unique tools for liberation of the human potential. Her work has helped thousands of people all over the world to free themselves from pain. You can find more about her at www.thejourney.com Page...

***Confirmation** is a learning period, ending with a ritual and a party for young people within the protestant church. Page...

***Contradiction knot.** Such knots occur in our psyche when we have to deal with two value systems, usually when our own childlike, trusting and loving soul meets educational or lazy parents who do not understand the child's mindset. Page...

*Coupling.** When we make a "system" in our inner being by connecting a feeling of something specific, either to a different feeling or to specific action or situations, it is called a coupling in this book. Page...

*Energy system** ensures that thoughts, feelings and ethereal energy are connected to the physical body. Thoughts and feelings vibrate in energy channels (also called chakras) and fields. When an energy channel is completely or partially closed because of emotional pain, physical pain occurs in the body. The direction of vibration starts in the heart, where the soul has its center. It vibrates both forwards and backwards, upwards and downwards from the middle of the chest. Then it splits into the entire energy field and vibrates inwards toward the body in the other energy channels. Pages...

*Gordian knot.** The expression has its origin from the time of Alexander the great. When he came to the city of Gordion and was asked to solve an unsolvable knot, he cut it with the cut of his sword. It isn't as simple as that in our psyche. I call it a Gordian knot when we carry a wound from a situation when we had a positive intention/experience that got a tragic/negative outcome. To release it, we need to say out loud both the positive intention and the negative outcome in the same sentence. Page...

*Helen Wambach.** American psychiatrist. The book «Life before life» (1982) describes the results of a study where she led a huge number of people at several different places and at different times into a trance back to the time of birth and before birth. The book contains some very interesting and vivid descriptions from different people about how it is to be born and thoughts the soul had both before and after the time of birth. Page...

***John Bradshaw** is an American author. Homepage: www.johnbradshaw.com Page...

***Kinesiology** means study of movement and is developed in the US as a fusion of the Western world's knowledge and philosophy, and the oriental world's knowledge about meridians and acupuncture points. (Source: Norwegian Kinesiology Association website, www.dnkf.org) Kinesiology retrieves information from the cells by testing the strength of the muscles in order to find the cause of pain and illness.

***Meridian system** is the finely divided part of the energy system that vibrates in the body from the cells back to the chest.

***Parallel event.** A parallel event is an event that has occurred as a result of repetitive thought patterns so that the creative energy in the subconscious (the cells from old wounds) activates similar feelings.

***Pendulum.** A pendulum is in this context a noble stone or a piece of jewelry hanging on a chain or a thread. The pendulum swings seemingly by itself because it is governed by energies we cannot see. It swings in certain ways for the individual and can provide answers on behalf of the soul or the body's cells. Page...

***Projecting.** When we carry painful, suppressed feelings that we do not see or don't want to see in ourselves, gets us to become irritated and criticize, accuse or disparage others in our mind or verbally. Page...

***Quantitative research method** is used when gathering a larger body of information, comparing the information and then drawing universally valid conclusions. Page...

***Qualitative research method** is used when examining and describing people's experiences and lessons learned through interviews and observation and then drawing conclusions from what has been found. Page...

*Regression. A trip back across time and space using relaxation methods, so that we are in our souls understanding and experience yet present in our waked mind. We can travel to fetal life, childhood, youth and adult life. We can also travel to past lives. Page...

*Release. To release means to set free our soul from emotional pain through recognising it, forgiveness and love so that we can let go of what hurts. Page...

*The Rosen Method. Touching combined with conversation are the tools of The Rosen Method. Deep touch and words are used to awaken the client's wondering, attention, being present in their body. By their hands and presence the therapist listens to the client's body signals. Tension is contacted in a soft, deep and direct way and the client's process is given careful attention. Page...

*Trauma – a very painful memory needed to be recognised and worked through in order to get a good life. It may be a memory you have put a lid on so that you can not remember it. Page...

Pictures for the book

Page 15: © Kenneth Kullman, Scandinavian Stockphoto
Page 25: © Dusan Zidar, Scandinavian Stockphoto
Page 39: © David Andor/Kenneth Lamøy
Page 50: © Inger Susaeg
Page 51: © Inger Susaeg
Page 56: © Phil Morley, Scandinavian Stockphoto
Page 74: © Syda Productions, Scandinavian Stockphoto
Page 85: © Tatiana Kostareva, Scandinavian Stockphoto
Page 105: © Madhourse, Scandinavian Stoskphoto
Page 120: © Carlos Soler Martinez/Scandinavian Stochphoto
Page 149: © Inger Susaeg

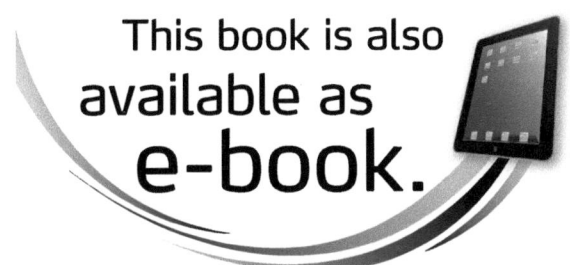

www.novum-publishing.co.uk

The author

Inger Susaeg was born in Oslo in 1951. She has higher education in art, music and drama. After working for nine years as assistant professor for drama at Bodø University, Norway, she left to pursue her passion for finding the answers to life's riddles. Her search led her to develop the Keys of Liberation. By using them thoroughly she developed expanded consciousness (enlightenment), meaning that she is able to seek answers by connecting to universal consciousness.

Today she offers lectures on her discoveries. Not only about how particles spin as soul and ethereal energy inside the body, but about how exploring the human psyche leads to many new possibilities for research within medicine, biology, phycology and physics. During recent years, she has discovered drama as a tool even when exploring existence. By giving people roles of being electrons and the task to form the structure of an atom, she discovered particles' conscious qualities.

novum PUBLISHER FOR NEW AUTHORS

The publisher

He who stops getting better stops being good.

This is the motto of novum publishing, and our focus is on finding new manuscripts, publishing them and offering long-term support to the authors.
Our publishing house was founded in 1997, and since then it has become THE expert for new authors and has won numerous awards.

Our editorial team will peruse each manuscript within a few weeks free of charge and without obligation.

You will find more information about
novum publishing and our books on the internet:

w w w . n o v u m - p u b l i s h i n g . c o . u k